# Life as an OxyMoron

**ox.y.mo.ron**—(ok se mò ron) *n. oxy—sharp, keen; moron—foolish, without intelligence*—A figure of speech in which opposite or contradictory ideas are combined.

Copyright © 2002 Rachel M. Mouton
United States of America

All rights reserved. This book may not be reproduced by electronic or mechanical means, without permission in writing from the author, with the exception of small excerpts.

Cover graphic artist; Steve Schneider

Copyright © 2005 Rachel M. Mouton
All rights reserved.
ISBN: 0-9744576-0-4

To order additional copies, please contact us.
BookSurge, LLC
www.booksurge.com
1-866-308-6235
orders@booksurge.com

# Life as an OxyMoron

## A perspective on paradoxes of lifestyle

Rachel M. Mouton

2005

# Life as an OxyMoron

## A perspective on paradoxes of lifestyle

Rachel M. Mouton

2005

# Life as an OxyMoron

*To my parents Lela & Whitney Mouton with love...*

# PRELUDE

This book comes from my heart. I dedicate it to my parents Lela and Whitney Mouton in honor of their unconditional love, support and guidance. Mom and Dad, thank you for all the years of hard work, fervent prayer and the many sacrifices you made for all of your children. Your benevolence and active lives in the church are true testaments of your goodness and faith. Words cannot express how much I love you and how grateful I am to God for granting me such wonderful parents. I know that you may not always agree with my drastic views, still I thank you for always challenging me to think for myself.

To my son Nicholas, never forget that you are the joy of my life and the strength, which has sustained me. Thank you for rising to the occasion of man of the house at such a young age. Remember that whatever you want in life, you've got to be willing to stick it out through the highs and lows, and not let other things deter you or let people discourage you.

To my sisters and brothers, Joan, Pete, Carl, Adrienne, Angela, Etta and Mark, the laughter and mischief of our tumultuous yesteryears will never be forgotten.

And to our children: Danielle, Byron, John, Adonis, Bryce, Peter Jeremy (P.J.), Terrance, Marcus, Nicholas, Desiree, Julia, Catrina, Crystal, Cash, Derrick, Valerie, Damien, Jeremy David (J.D.), Chincie, Brian Keith (B.K.) and Jordan, this is my gift to you and your children. May it transcend through time and serve as a reflection of your family's love for you and as evidence of your colorful lineage and Christian heritage. By the world's standards it won't seem like much of an heirloom; but I pray at least that it points *you* to treasures of the richest kind.

To my extended family…keep the faith, literally.

And to all who read this, may it touch your spirit and lift you to a new level of awareness about your own life…as an oxymoron.

In a world that so often reveres money, power, and fame, undoubtedly, there are many who may feel that their lives are not particularly noteworthy. Yet to the extent that *all* life is worthy, we may *all* have a little something that is at least worth noting. This is my perspective. It is a perspective on the many contradicting values of life…and in my life, fusing race and religion was among the first.

I discovered the world from a small town in southwest Louisiana during a time when the Christian concepts we learned often produced stark contrasts to the reality of our every day lives. Within the confines of our parochial school system, Colored children were taught by caring nuns, White missionaries from the north and other far off places. The Sisters that lived in our community were completely dedicated to our Christian education. Through them and our parish priest, we learned that we were loved in God's eyes.

Beyond the playful laughter of our Catholic school ground and church, just a few streets down and across the tracks was another Catholic school and church established just for Whites. Their large brick facilities were noticeably nicer, much more stately than our modest wooden structures, but even more noticeable was that intermingling between their establishment and ours was non-existent. We were all Christians of one faith, in one town, worshiping one God, but we couldn't have been more separate. We were all taught from the same Bible that we were to love our neighbors as ourselves, yet the clear lines of racial separation prevailed. We all sang the song verse from our hymn booklet, "We are one in the Spirit, we are one in the Lord" but we sang it from separate pews in separate churches. So regardless of the motions everyone was going through, as far as I could see, there was no real oneness and no real unity of faith in our little town.

When I was in third grade, Sister Isaac Jogues decided to walk our class across town to the little public library. Sister Isaac was young, pretty, and freckled-faced with big soft eyes. Just a hint of her golden red hair was visible in front of her veil. What comfortable life had she and the other nuns given up to live with us in this small, hot, dusty town while local Whites seemed intent on distancing themselves from us as much as possible? I sometimes wondered. Yet, here they were, so natural with us, exuding nothing but love, discipline, and an ardent desire to teach.

Taking us to the library was a bold move on Sister's part. I vividly recall the resistance she encountered from the librarian as we waited outside the door. Sister Isaac would not back down. She knew there was no just reason why Colored children couldn't check out books at a public library. We didn't know. That look of *you don't belong here* was all too familiar to us, even at that young age. We learned quickly that Whites had a strong sense of entitlement that we were not privy to. Not to our surprise, the librarian resolved that each child would be required to have an adult sign to be responsible for the books; of course our parents were nowhere in sight. Sister Isaac gladly accepted the responsibility and signed for each of our books as we were allowed to go into the library a few at a time.

The library was among the first of many venues we were introduced to by the nuns as they pressed against a path of resistance. Just as it was on this particular day, our class was returning from another little outing. I remember it was scorching hot and we were strolling and singing along to keep our minds off the heat when a station wagon pulled up and a White woman asked Sister Isaac if she needed a ride. Sister glanced around at us to see if we could all fit in the air-conditioned wagon that had just presented itself. She asked the driver, "Do you think we can all fit?" Suddenly the woman's whole face changed and it became quite apparent that her cool offer did not include us. The expression on Sister's face changed too. She was appalled at this woman who expected her to leave a bunch of young children to walk alone on a busy street and in so many words Sister told her so. As you can probably imagine, that was the end of that.

On another occasion, while at school, Mother Jude, our Mother Superior, reprimanded us for yelling, "There's a White man at the door." She told us that she didn't care what color he was and that in the future we should say, "There's a gentleman at the door." Prefacing people by color was not something we had invented. Besides, had she no idea how easy it was to reciprocate prejudice? Even if we didn't know what the word meant, to children it translated as rejection and hatred. Yet somehow, despite this projected translation, our teachers were White and they were raising the bar for us. Using little more than tattered books, rudimentary tools, and lots of discipline, they transformed our little school into an accelerated learning environment. The Sisters taught us to rise above the subtle and not-so-subtle cruelties around us, to overlook the differences, how differently we looked, and how differently we were being treated. It didn't matter if someone from the other race was calling us "dumb niggers," we were expected to be well-mannered, intelligent children of God. Of course, this was hard for young kids to accept, but, like many things to come in life, we learned to work around the disparities. And as long as everyone respected the unwritten lines in place, people were basically friendly and got along just fine in our little town.

Without a doubt, these life lessons were confusing and

painful. Strangely, they proved to be only chapter one of what I was to learn on skin color. To my surprise and much to my chagrin, I was soon aware that a similar dichotomy existed within the so-called boundaries of my own race and culture. Colored children were quickly categorized by the shade of their skin and the grade of their hair. This kind of differentiating was also being passed on from generation to generation. Oh, I'm sure that with some people this learned behavior was carried out in jest, but for others, it was much more serious than that.

Hair that was a finer texture, closer to that of White people's hair, was called "good." Good hair generally meant that you didn't have to undergo the treacherous ritual of using a hot comb or chemicals to make your bad hair look good. Bad hair was kinky, bushy, unruly, and bluntly referred to as a "nappy head." So, not only were Colored children subjected to racial slurs from another race, some had to deal with attacks on their self-esteem from within their own race. You see, in a very tangible way, Colored children were being taught that something they inherited was inherently *bad*.

Next on the measuring scale was whether or not a child was light-skinned or dark-skinned, and with our little colloquial twist, these were pronounced "light skin-ded" and "dark skin-ded." Having lighter skin was much more favorable for similar reasons that you'd rather have good hair; the more White-looking the better. And if someone was described as a *bright* person, it had nothing to do with intelligence, a radiant smile, or anything substantive, it was just more surface rhetoric about skin. Ironically, this was the same preoccupation that the Black race had been trying to overcome with the White race in this country since slavery…people judging people by mere appearances…people judging people by the color of their skin.

# THEY'LL KNOW WE ARE CHRISTIANS BY OUR LOVE

We are one in the Spirit, we are one in the Lord
We are one in the Spirit, we are one in the Lord
And we pray that all unity may one day be restored
And they'll know we are Christians by our love
By our love, yes they'll know we are Christians by our love

We will walk with each other, we will walk hand in hand
We will walk with each other, we will walk hand in hand
And together we'll spread the news that God is in our land
And they'll know we are Christians by our love
By our love, yes they'll know we are Christians by our love

We will work with each other, we will work side by side
We will work with each other we will work side by side
And we'll guard people's dignity and save each person's pride
And they'll know we are Christians by our love
By our love, yes they'll know we are Christians by our love

Source: Church Hymn Missalette

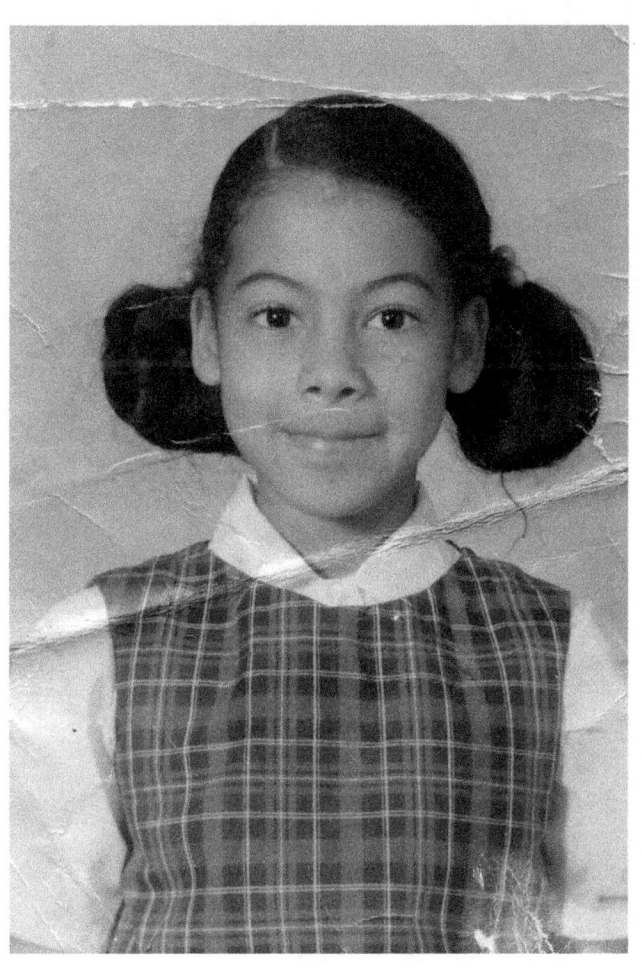

*me...*

*Sister Isaac Jogues with Third & Fourth Grade Classes*

*Playing Volley Ball with Sister Isaac Jogues*

## THANK YOU

To my Heavenly Father, thank you for today
A heavenly day for we have lost count of time
Cheerful laughter in the midst of the air
Thank you for today...knowing you were there.
Loosing ourselves in your warm embrace
Today I felt you were with us and no other place.
As the night grew nearer, still with no sorrow
I rest my head knowing you will be there tomorrow.

Written by my brother,
Peter W. Mouton

The times I was recalling earlier, were the late 60's and almost proved too much for a little caramel-colored, bright-eyed, bushy-pig-tailed girl to absorb, especially since the complexion of my family, spanned from Irish Cream to Island Mocha. The more extended family you met, the broader that spectrum got…each one remarkably different…all somehow remarkably beautiful. We were a lot like a field of wildflowers. No single wildflower is lovelier than the next; rather it's in the uniqueness of each that collectively the field displays its beautiful tapestry.

My mom's sister, Aunt Rita, once told us a heartwarming story about something that happened years ago when she took our Great Aunt Lena to the little neighborhood grocery store that they frequented. Aunt Lena was a tiny, sturdy woman in her seventies with lots of spunk. She had translucent vanilla skin and long gray hair, which she wore pulled back in a bun. Everyone in the neighborhood, Black and White, knew and loved her. During that time, there was a lot of ruckus surrounding the racial integration of public schools. A few White women were openly discussing how they felt about it as Aunt Lena approached the counter. Poking a little fun with her, one of them said, "Huh, Aunt Leen, what do you think about all this integration stuff?" Aunt Lena slowly rolled up her sleeve, pointed to her pale forearm and retorted, "You see this…we've been integrating for a long time!"

Yes, great, Aunt Lena, I'm sure the double standards were painstakingly obvious, and some still are today.

It was years later before I understood that Colored people in Louisiana could be mixed with almost anything. In my extended family alone, from my mother's side and my father's, the blood of the African American, West Indian, Native American, French, and Irish all run through our veins. Long ago, society dictated that *Negro* blood mixed with anything else made you Colored. There were obvious disadvantages with such a label.

Cocktails of this sort are not at all uncommon for people of Louisiana. Through the years a lot of labels have been fashioned to decipher the different blends, again mostly by the degree of Black blood one had in them. *Mulattos* are people who are half-Black and half-White. In the south, when I was coming up, Mulattos and other Colored people who looked White were sometimes accused of *passing* for White, but not to their faces of course. Passing meant they were pretending to be White in certain settings for certain conveniences. Before you start to judge, try to imagine that you are Colored during the 40's, 50's, or 60's and things are pretty segregated and you are going to see the only doctor in town, who of course is White, and you have the choice of sitting in an air-conditioned waiting room with cushy seats and magazines to read or sitting on hard folding chairs in a hot stuffy hallway in the back. Which one would you choose? Or, try to imagine that you're in desperate need of work to support your family and you know that your only chance of being hired is if you check off the 'White' box on the job application for your race. In fact, life in general would be much easier and the world much kinder if you could just be White. From my perspective, I never figured out if passing made someone a sell-out to their race or a buy-in to the system. I guess like most things, it's a matter of perspective.

Another thing that some Mulattos and light-skinned Colored people were quietly accused of was that they were *color-struck* for not wanting to mingle with or marry folks who were dark-complected. Again, with the heavy accent of the local people, the term was more often pronounced "color-stroke." Intentional or not, merging the word *color* with *stroke* in a place with a pigmentation preoccupation conjured up some very amusing images.

Some sources claim that Mulattos considered themselves neither Black nor White, so it was nothing personal. How could they be neither when they were both? You see, the whole scenario presented quite an uncomfortable paradox for everyone concerned. From my humble perspective, if Mulattos were color-struck, this meant they resented or rejected the very thing that shaped their *off-White* culture in the first place: the blending of color.

Next, there was a more inclusive term that was widely used: *Creole.* It attempted to capture most of Louisiana's eclectic mix as a people, a language, and a cuisine. Even this all-encompassing word and its proper usage gave cause for contention. Reportedly, some of the pure descendants of French and Spanish people were adamant that the term Creole did not include Blacks. What did they think this was, some kind of exclusive country club or something?

The term Creole was and still is used in other parts of the world by locals to describe their native blends of people; its use is not reserved for Louisiana. In fact, persons with some European parentage born in the West Indies, Central America, and tropical South America are also called Creoles in those countries. Furthermore, the multi-colored face of the melted Black race of Louisiana does not need a stamp of approval to know that it is a vital part of the Creole mix. Although the controversy, Creole is widely used today to describe *any* mix of descendants of Spanish, French, African, and West Indian settlers in the Louisiana area. The Native Americans who were already rooted here, often go unaccounted for, but their blood too is an integral part of this mix.

Despite all the baffling signals surrounding skin color, my

early years proved to be joyful and adventurous. We were a big close-knit family. My parents had eight children and they were loving, hard working people. They were very involved in our upbringing and spent a lot of quality time with us kids when they weren't working, and they worked a lot. And I can still remember that exciting day when we moved into our new brick home with a great big yard; we're talking two acres of land here, filled with pecan and fruit trees, cumquats, figs, pears, and persimmons, some of which could be preserved for the winter. There was also an enormous China Ball tree that gave soothing shade to our swing set and at the same time provided our mischievous brothers with an unlimited supply of ammo for their slingshots. But the trees I remember most of all are the tall pine trees because of their earthy cones and the never-ending job of raking pine needles.

Our father, Whitney, loved to whistle as he worked out in the yard or garden. He would hear a song on the radio early in the morning, then all day long he would blow this sweet, silky tune. I can't explain it exactly, but it gave me a warm, safe feeling as a little girl. He built us a playhouse and, for those sweltering hot summers, Daddy would set up the swimming pool. In those days, we played jacks, jumped rope, and hopscotch for hours with the neighborhood kids. Every Christmas we were showered with toys and gifts followed by a big holiday dinner with all the trimmings. It truly was a wonderful life. Of course, as kids we had no idea that by the nation's social order, we were considered poor. To us, we were rich; we had everything!

Our parents shared in all the responsibilities from cooking and cleaning to taking care of and taxiing us kids around. Daddy was an industrious man with a tremendous work ethic, always juggling several jobs. Even at home he was rarely idle, except for watching a good cowboy movie, the Ed Sullivan or the

Red Skelton Show. He liked the way that Red said, "God bless" at the end of every show. Daddy worked for the parish school board, driving a school bus for nearly thirty years. In the early part of those years, in the mornings and evenings, he also cleaned the local bank and post office as side gigs. In between those jobs, he would cook for his family, tend to his cattle, and work in his garden. Daddy also had seasonal work as a headwaiter at night in a restaurant at the local horse racetrack, eventually becoming Maitre de. He'd get in late, but sometimes on Friday nights we could stay up late and he'd bring us leftover treats and empty his pockets of the tips he'd collected for us to split between us, and boy did we scramble to collect them.

My father and his brothers and buddies worked with their hands a lot, dabbling in everything from mechanics to electrical work to carpentry. It wasn't unusual that Daddy had a couple of rental houses built for fun and the added income.

It's hard to admit now, but I use to think that my father was passive around Whites because he was always so polite to them, even in those early years when he didn't always get respect in return. I would think of him on his feet late at night in that restaurant waiting on them, saying "yes, Sir" to their every request, even if their request ended with "boy." Now I know my daddy was far from faultless, but I would bet my bottom dollar that he had more character in his little pinky than most of those *honkies* had in their entire beings. It wasn't until I grew up that I understood my father's approach a lot better. I believe he genuinely liked all people and usually gave everyone the benefit of the doubt. Through the years, this earned him many friends, both Black and White. It turns out that Daddy wasn't passive after all; he just never lost sight of his objective. He was making the most out of what was available to a Black man without a college education in the south. He did what he had to do with dignity.

He may not have had a 'high-falutin' job with a fancy title, but he was definitely hardworking and a smart businessman. Daddy's drive and collective efforts drew an income that allowed his family to live very well and his children never wanted for anything.

## CHILDREN LEARN WHAT THEY LIVE

If children live with criticism, they learn to condemn
If children live with hostility, they learn to fight
If children live with ridicule, they learn to be shy
If children live with shame, they learn to feel
guilty
If children live with tolerance, they learn to be patient
If children live with encouragement, they learn confidence
If children live with acceptance, they learn to appreciate
If children live with fairness, they learn justice
If children live with security, they learn to have faith
If children live with kindness, they learn to love in the world.

-author unknown-

Our mother, Lela worked the graveyard shift at a local hospital. She had attended traditionally Black schools, Holy Rosary Institute and Southern Institute. Mama started out as a nurse's aid, then became an LPN, eventually specializing in private duty nursing. She made quite a name for herself with some of the more affluent Whites in the surrounding communities, those who could afford to have nurses care for their elderly in the privacy of their homes. There was no doubt about it, Mama loved her work and she must have been good at it because her services were always in demand. Sometimes though, we kids overheard dreadful stories about incidents that had occurred while she was in their homes. Of course, if we were caught listening to adult conversation, Mama would quickly convert from speaking in English to French. Even with that being the case, through the years, we still managed to pick up quite a few of these stories. Later on in life, I would come to refer to them as little *Driving Miss Daisy* episodes.

Our mother was educated, competent, and witty. Sometimes her older, White patients still expected her to do housekeeping or take them to the grocery store or beauty parlor in addition to her regular duties. Mama didn't mind. Our family knew, however, that the little innuendos and racial slurs she sometimes heard were offensive. One elderly patient even had the audacity to tell my mother that she shouldn't be eating her meals at the same time as her. The woman told my mother to wait until she was finished eating, then it would be appropriate for my mother to eat. My mother was a nurse, not an indentured servant. Thank goodness all of her patients were not like this. She developed special bonds with many of them. I'm sure that through the years she felt less like a domestic and more like a nurse. Still, this other stuff really bothered us new generation of kids.

What about all the other Black women who, for years, walked long distances in worn down shoes to cook for and clean up after Whites for just pennies? I can't tell you how many times I secretly wished that I could dispel all the rooty-tooty notions that I presumed Whites had about these women; women who were forced to take on subservient roles and leave their own children at home to go and care for White children. Specifically, when it came to my mom, I wanted all those "Miss Daisy's" to know that when she left their homes after working ten to twelve hour shifts, she went home to a loving family in a beautiful house, not that much unlike theirs, and inside all the comforts and amenities that they enjoyed. We may not have had a lot of fancy collectables, but we had nice things. One of our best treasures hung in the middle of our living room, a beautiful framed message proudly boasting, *"Choose you this day whom ye will serve;. . .as for me and my household, we will serve the Lord."—Joshua 24:15*

On occasion, we would ask our mother how she endured those uncomfortable moments. We found out in so many words that she, like so many people of color, had learned to ignore the rude actions of others rather than be provoked. In the same way that we were learning as kids, I surmised, but under more intense grown-up conditions. Besides, Mama was a very faith-filled woman. She embraced her work as a ministry, not just a job, and, believe it or not, she really loved her patients. Eventually, I concluded that if some of them wanted to hang on to their bigotry with one foot on a banana peel and the other one on the grave, then so be it. It was their shortcoming, not hers. Somehow, Mama never let any of this hinder the care and compassion she gave them. I grew to love and respect her so much more than

I already had for that. I wish that more of her patients and their families could have read the poem my mom wrote about caring for them, *Who am I Lord?* Perhaps then they might have appreciated her for the spiritually compassionate woman that she was and still is.

## WHO AM I, LORD?

Who am I Lord to try and do
What feeble hands were accustomed to
I cannot take the pride away
That you give them Lord, day by day

But let my goal in this life be
Only to help whenever I see
Assistance is needed with a task
That humble pride won't let them ask

Send them not suffering they can't bear
Let me assure them lest they despair
That you always have them in Your care
Give them courage Lord as they age
Be mindful of the souls You made

And when this stage in life I come
that daily routines are not easily done
Please send me someone who will understand
to help…assure…not give command.

Written by my mother,
Lela Gordon Mouton

As a teenager, I was very inquisitive with somewhat of a defiant spirit. I no longer felt obligated to take what adults told me at face value, especially since I had already witnessed the contradiction between the words and ways of many. Not to mention that often with adults when you asked them if you could do something, the response "no" didn't come with explanation. "No" simply meant "no" and asking "why not," was predictably followed by, "because I said so." So, like many teenagers, I usually delved in and drew my own conclusions about things. I was a bit experimental and took some chances. Since I am not or ever will be the leader of the free world, I guess it is safe to say that I *did* inhale. I am not bragging about this, but as a free thinker, I never cared much for conformity, especially when there was no understanding of why you could do or not do something. Even though I had respect for tradition, it appeared that things were done a certain way just for the sake of convention.

In the 70's, people kept track of things like if a school was predominantly Black or predominantly White and I was determined to be no less than anyone else at a predominantly White high school. My parents encouraged us kids to participate in extra-curricular activities. I ambitiously immersed myself in almost everything: cheerleading, student council, honor societies, and clubs galore. It didn't once dawn on me back then how much my parents had to sacrifice to pay for these extras for all their children. Probably because I was a bit prideful and not sensitive enough to realize that many Blacks in our town probably could not afford these things.

Throughout high school, I occasionally received awards and honors, but the award I cherished most was one I had received a few years earlier. It was the Optimist Club Award and it left an indelible impression on my heart. I remember innocently rushing home to look up the word, *optimist*, in the dictionary to make sure I could live up to exactly what it meant. Imagine my surprise when I learned that I had just been honored for having a cheerful disposition and a hopeful outlook on life. I remember naively thinking back then, now what could possibly be easier than that.

In those days, when Blacks were involved in extra stuff at a predominantly White school, it automatically meant interacting more with Whites. I didn't think a lot about it; I gradually began to associate with Whites and Blacks alike. Sooner or later, I found out that this wasn't always a comfortable place to be. If you hung around with Whites or carried yourself a certain way, other Blacks would accuse you of *acting White* or you might be labeled an *Oreo*. That's right. The name of a famous cookie was used as a metaphor for someone who was Black on the outside and White on the inside. Essentially, you were being called a traitor. To add insult to injury, when I ran into some of my White, so-called friends in the mall or at a restaurant, it was a toss up as to whether or not they would even acknowledge me. Those few seconds between seeing and possibly greeting always flustered me. After a few rejections, I stopped looking for their acknowledgements and began turning the other way first, just not to have to deal with it. Gradually I learned the difference between acquaintanceship and true friendship and the difference between just being courteous and actually caring about someone. I also discovered that deep within my heart I was capable of hurting…and hating.

Every year the school held a beauty ball, a formal dance and contest. In my junior year, six Black girls out of thirty were selected to be sweetheart contestants in the pageant-like ceremony.

The rest of the contestants were White. This was the first time a Black would be elected beauty ball queen at our school. What could the White panel of judges have been thinking? *Me*.... chosen among a string of mostly White girls! I could see the surprise on everyone's faces and I couldn't mask my shock. I didn't know if I had won by some split-vote fluke or if I was truly the intended pick, but at that moment it really didn't matter. You see, up to that moment, much of life around me had suggested that White girls were prettier, smarter, and better than Black girls somehow. That kind of conditioning is hard to reverse, but my tiara and full academic scholarship were definitely a good start. Fortunately, a couple of years later, I stumbled across the most compelling *beauty tips* from a surprising source and these helped me to put physical beauty into a proper perspective.

## BEAUTY TIPS

For attractive lips, speak words of kindness
For lovely eyes, seek out the good in people
For a slim figure, share your food with the hungry
For beautiful hair, let a child run his or her fingers through it once a day
For poise, walk with the knowledge that you
never walk alone.

People even more than things, have to be restored, renewed, revived, reclaimed and redeemed. Never throw out anybody. Remember if you ever need a helping hand, you'll find one at the end of your arm. As you grow older, you will discover that you have two hands, one for helping yourself and the other for helping others.

The beauty of a woman is not in the clothes she wears, the figure she carries, or the way she combs her hair. The beauty of a woman must be seen from in her eyes, because that is the doorway to her heart, the place where love is.
The beauty of a woman is not in a facial mole,
but true beauty in a woman is reflected in her soul.

It is the caring that she lovingly gives, the passion she shows, and the true beauty of a woman with passing years—only grows!

**Audrey Hepburn**

In the late 70's, I attended Dillard University in New Orleans, a traditionally Black university. Everyone was Black; administrators, teachers, and students. It was there that I learned to understand and truly be proud of my Black heritage. Not only did I learn more about great, historical, Black figures, but I was meeting some present-day ones. Some of my classmates were from affluent families, middle class as *they* say. They were sometimes referred to as bourgeois. Not coincidently, it was right about this time that I added a new phrase to my vocabulary: *bourgey Negro*.

A few semesters later, I transferred back home. I hated to leave the city but for reasons too many to go in to, I enrolled at the University of Southwestern Louisiana in the neighboring town of Lafayette. My mother's sister had been the first African-American to graduate from this university.

College life was drastically different from high school to me. I didn't join any clubs or even pledge with a sorority. I'd had enough of extra- curricular activities for a while and wanted simply to enjoy my freedom, freedom to set my own schedule, freedom to come and go as I pleased.

After college life, stepping into the real world meant moving to a big city for me. There was a great big world out there and I wanted a piece of it so I leapt right in. It was undoubtedly the most eager and unsuspecting time of my life.

San Francisco in the early 80's was full of chaos and wonder, skyscrapers, sandy shores, art galleries, theatres and concerts, professional sports, and on and on. Every day brought a new occasion for me to learn and experience more about life. I was meeting people from all walks of life, people with different customs and different beliefs. It was fascinating. If you've never been exposed to people from other parts of the world, you can easily have misconceptions about them and their differences. It was amazing how many people I met from remote places who believed that because I was from Louisiana, I should know a little something about voodoo. However, I knew as little as they did. I knew of the pin-doll.

Surprisingly, the more I got to know people and the more I was around different kinds of people, the more I realized that intrinsically, we're all the same. Some people are good, some not so good, but this has nothing to do with extrinsic traits. For the first time in my life, it was astounding to see people of every race and nationality living and working together. Inter-racial and inter-cultural relationships were out in the open and appeared to be generally accepted. I'm sure racial hang-ups did exist; they just weren't as blatant as in a small southern town. It didn't take me long to learn though, that city life had its own collage of contradictions to contend with.

I entered the corporate world with much vigor and approached my work as I had my studies. I figured it would be about as mechanical as school was for me—I studied hard, got good grades and I graduated. I would work hard, get good reviews, and get promoted. I didn't think there were that many other variables in the mix. As you can see I was textbook smart, not real world savvy. This would change though very quickly, and my training would begin on the very first day as I encountered the inquisitive nature of those who'd been vying for the marketing job for which I had just been hired; a great job with Chevron Oil Company.

After years in the corporate world and exposure to other companies, my views changed. As far as moving up the ladder of success, what I once believed would be healthy competition turned out to be more like cut-throat-ition. Being a quick study, I'd already picked up the daily jargon of the grind, including the classics: backstabbing, brown-nosing, and sleeping-your-way-to-the-top. My new vernacular was jam-packed with 'isms'…click-ism, favoritism, nepotism, token-ism and sexism to go along with the already well understood racism. I discovered that a good team player was someone who didn't make waves, but one who was expected to go with the flow of things, even if it streamed toward the side of injustice. Consistently bucking the system would only earn you the title "loose cannon," after which you were sure to be assigned to something nebulous and dispensable like "special projects." With just a little O.J.T., in no time flat I knew how to M.Y.O.B. and C.Y.A. on the J.O.B. just to stay in the game. I was mildly successful, but learning the ropes of corporate America did not live up to my idealized notion of a career path.

There were many eye openers along the way to teach me about real life and how it differed dramatically from my early quixotic views. The events that stand out in my mind were those that presented a direct conflict with the ideals instilled in me from my youth.

Later in my career, I worked for an information systems company, National Data Corporation in Atlanta, GA. I remember one day, I'd just returned from lunch and headed to the conference room for a meeting. I was quietly telling one of my cohorts that, while I was walking, I saw a woman and her two children begging on the street. The kids were holding a cardboard sign that read "need money for food," so I stopped and gave them some money. Before I could finish getting my thought out, another co-worker blurted out, "You're silly. She always works that street and she probably makes more money than you do in a day. Her kids won't even eat after she buys her booze and drugs." Suddenly, almost everyone in the room was laughing and I became really angered by their intrusion. More so, I think I was angry at the idea that people I surrounded myself with everyday, thought I was gullible for trying to help someone. It wasn't that I didn't have a sense of humor or that I felt taken, I just couldn't see anything funny about that family's predicament. Responding firmly, I said, "I don't care what she does with the money. I gave it out of the goodness of my heart." Suddenly the room was conspicuously quiet and, much to my relief, the meeting began.

During the meeting, while the V.P. of Service was babbling on about unbundling services so that we could charge our customers more for delivering the same thing as before, my mind began to wander. *I don't have to explain to my co-workers why I choose to care about other human beings.* I was no saint, so it wasn't like I was trying to be holier-than-thou. Even if I were, I wouldn't have jumped into a spill about, *'whatsoever you do to the least of your brothers'* because I'd already figured out that it was politically incorrect to bring your faith into the workplace…. an incongruous dilemma in itself. Nevertheless, I was getting sick and tired of people misconstruing nice for naïve. I admit, I probably was still a bit green about the ways of the world, but I refused to accept genuine kindness as a weakness. Helping others came naturally to me. When it didn't, I worked at it. Through the example of my parents and early teachers, I knew that Christianity was supposed to be a *way of life,* not just a religion. This way of life was based on a very simple premise: *do unto others as you would have them do unto you*; a premise that is often lost in the battle of egos competing for title, power, and money. This may be somewhat judgmental, but many of these corporate types only did something demonstrably charitable during the United Way Drive or at Christmas time. The rest of the time their actions, or should

I say inactions, demonstrated that they viewed good deeds as a nuisance and good deeds done for strangers was considered downright dangerous.

Without a doubt, that whole incident affected me more than I cared to admit. It reminded me of that empty feeling I got whenever I saw someone stranded on the side of a road, long before cell phones became popular. In those first three seconds, I instinctively wanted to help, but with just a few seconds more, reasoning would kick in to remind me that the world just wasn't safe enough to stop and offer a helping hand to another human being. Like most people, I just rolled on by. The next time I saw the beggar, I started to just walk on by. Curiosity got the best of me or maybe I didn't want to feel the *cold within*. I glanced back and caught a glimpse of her kids. They were unkempt, but so precious. I could just see the sadness in their eyes. I bought hamburgers for them and gave the woman a little change.

# THE COLD WITHIN

Six humans trapped by happenstance in dark and bitter cold,
each one possessed a stick of wood or so the story's told.
Their dying fire in need of logs, the first woman held hers back,
for on the faces around the fire, she noticed one was Black.

The next man looking across the way saw one not of his church
and couldn't bring himself to give the fire his stick of birch.
The third one sat in tattered clothes. He gave his coat a hitch.
Why should his log be put to use, to warm the idle rich?

The rich man just sat back and thought of the wealth he had in store,
and how to keep what he had earned from the lazy, shiftless poor.

The Black man's face bespoke revenge as the fire passed from his sight.
For all he saw in his stick of wood was a chance to spite the White.

And the White man of this forlorn group did naught except for gain.
Giving only to those who gave to him was how he played the game.
The logs held tight in death's still hands was proof of human sin
They didn't die from the cold without, they died from the cold within

-author unknown-

There was nothing in my early years to prepare me for the enormous shift in the way I would come to look at the world over time; not even racism had prepared me for its coldness and hardness. Nothing in my sheltered childhood prepared me for the nature of some people—people with all sorts of hidden motives and agendas. This was the darker side of life where I had to learn to separate the lambs from the wolves dressed in sheep's clothing. Even on the transit ride to work, I had to learn to look out for pickpockets getting too close, con artists peddling genuine-imitation stuff, and all sorts of other 'city slickers' perpetrating as well-intentioned people.

I was no innocent *Rebecca of Sunny Brook Farm*, but I didn't know how to deal with people at *this* level and honestly, I didn't know if I wanted to. Compassion and integrity were treasured values to me, even if I strayed from them at times. There just wasn't much room for that kind of stuff in the big league where the games were played by masters. And, nowhere were they played better than in the dating scene where pursuers resorted to all kinds of pretentious behavior to impress, manipulate and seduce one another. Sadly in the end, even breaking someone's heart could be considered a feat to gloat over with your cronies. When you're exposed to that kind of artificiality every day, it's hard not to get caught up in the farce. You can either play or get played. After a while, it's hard to know, hard to trust, hard to love, and hard to just keep it real.

Just about the time I was beginning to accept life for what it was, the good, the bad, and the ugly, death came knocking at my door, taking someone very close to me. Trying to get a handle on life is one thing, but death, now that is entirely another.

Death rearranged my existence quickly and dramatically. This new dimension of loss introduced feelings of melancholy that I had never known before; creating a kind of hollowness deep within me, the likes of which I never knew existed.

There is nothing like death to make you think of your mistakes and what you could have done differently. There is nothing like death to make you face your own mortality…ashes to ashes and dust to dust. There is nothing like death to cause you to want to believe in eternal life. Yet there is nothing like death to make you angry with God. It's cold and dark and awkward enough when it happens to elderly people of natural causes, but it's mercilessly wretched when death comes unexpectedly, leaving many unanswered questions.

People felt obliged to say, "time heals all" and "this too shall pass," but as time marched on, people kept recharging my sorrow. For me, it was a tough time to learn just how quick some people are to judge, as if any of them held the answers to life and death. All I know is that when I was at the lowest and most vulnerable point in my life, I saw the best and the worst side of people. If people are comfortable kicking you when you're down, imagine what they may be capable of doing when you're on top. Naturally, I became somewhat tentative and leery of outsiders and their true intentions. I withdrew to myself and was so sensitive at times that those close to me often felt like they had to walk on eggshells around me. If someone or something had set out to destroy my light and free spirit, it appeared as though they might be succeeding. But there's a funny thing about being at rock bottom…there's nowhere else to go but up.

Death would touch my life again and again, until I was forced to accept it as a part of life. As I worked through my trust issues, I began to let people back into my world. Over time, I found that I could tune into the 'vibes' I was getting from others, regardless of what they were doing or saying on the surface. It was a strange awareness, like having a built in tuning fork. It was almost as though I could see through people and straight to the heart of things. Today, I believe this to be a spiritual gift, a very useful one called discernment. For the time being though, it was an encumbering gift and cause for major adjustment in my life because, despite all that I'd seen and been through thus far, I still wanted to love and trust people. I learned, however, that whenever I ignored this insight, it always came back to bite me. So from this point going forward, there would be no more looking at life through rose-colored glasses, just *true colors* shining through.

    I had many blessings in my life to be grateful for, a progressive career, and supportive family, but still this God of endless power, mercy, and love I'd been taught to believe in as a child, seemed distant and foggy. Only fragments of what my religious faith had taught me seemed applicable to me in adult real life. Sometimes I would sit and ponder the point of it all. As time would drag on, it wasn't just my pain anymore, but the pain of all humanity that seemed more apparent than ever before. And I didn't have to go far to find it...just turn on the news and see people suffering and starving or fighting and killing, open a window and hear the sirens of trouble. It was so up close and personal that I could be dining at an elegant Ritz and after dinner cross the street and trip over a homeless person. I just wasn't sure anymore about this God of power who seemingly allowed such needless and senseless suffering. By now I'd learned to do what most people appeared to be able to master effortlessly: the art of *going through the motions* in life without questioning the obvious duplicity, without challenging the double standards that separate our principles from the way we carry out our lives. And I carried this guise for nearly a decade.

So this was the real world that I'd been so anxious to embrace, all decked out with its incongruities, cruelties, and man's indifference to it all. My experiences en toto had changed my outlook on life, changed my love for life, and changed me. I was learning a different code of ethics than the one I learned in Catholic school.... '*do onto others before they do it onto you.*'

And so it was, from my childhood, well into my adulthood, life offered more contradictions and contortions than continuity and clarity, not just in my personal life, but in life in general: people starving to death while tons of food are wasted, people destroying the earth while spending trillions to camp out on the moon, people taking prayer out of schools and allowing death to fill the cavity it created, people cloning life with little concern for creating life without a soul, our money saying 'in God we trust' while far too many trust in the money. And now, we sit back as cyber space and virtual reality take precedence over our living space and actual reality. *Why?*

# WHY?

Why do the babies starve,
when there's enough food to feed the world?
Why when there's so many of us,
are there people still alone?
Why are the missiles called peacekeepers
when they're aimed to kill?
Why is a woman still not safe,
when she's in her home?
Love is hate. War is peace. No is yes. And we're all free…
But somebody's gonna have to answer,
the time is coming soon
Amidst all these questions and contradictions,
there's some who seek the truth
Yes somebody's gonna have to answer,
the time is coming soon
When the blind remove their blinders
and the speechless speak the truth
Love is hate. War is peace. No is yes. But we're all free…

Song © 1988, Traci Chapman

The 90's crept up on me. There I was in my early thirties still *going through the motions* in life. My mind and my days were cluttered with schedules, obligations, and things-to-do lists. I did what was required of me to stay afloat, but there was a growing apathy about everything around me. Negative energy and a stressful lifestyle had taken their toll. One morning, I was stuck in traffic and my thoughts went in a very unusual way. I found myself asking "why am I here?" Not why am I here on this highway or why am I here in this city, but why am I here on this planet? I looked through my rear view mirror and gazed at miles of vehicles stopped in the early morning rush. There must have been thousands of us sitting in metal boxes on wheels, swarming over the earth. We were all hustling and bustling this day as we had done the day before and, like well-programmed robots, we would all come back and do it again tomorrow. Wasn't there more to life? I know this kind of thinking is weird and ethereal, even for someone like me. I don't know why on this particular morning, I couldn't just take in the view as I always had. After all, it was only rush hour traffic.

One evening shortly after that experience, I was feeling a bit disheartened again and decided to pray. This was more than I had done in recent years. Rather than reciting one of the many pre-written prayers I'd gathered over time, I knelt before my bed and prayed in my own words. I pleaded with God about the complacency in my life and my numbness of faith. I asked Him to allow me to feel His peace, His presence. That night, I wept until my pillow was nearly saturated and finally, at some God-forsaken hour, I fell asleep.

The next morning, sunrays were shooting in through the

bay windows of my bedroom and they had special warmth to them. As they fell upon me, I felt a sense of tranquility. Still groggy, I recalled my prayer of the night before and wondered if this could possibly be an answer. Then, I thought, either God works really fast or it's been a tremendously long time since I've been able to appreciate the soothing embrace of the sun. In either case, I laid there, practically motionless, for as long as I could, basking in the peaceful warm glow.

Time marched on, but I kept thinking about those blissful moments. I wished that I could have clung on to them forever. The everyday routine quickly brought me back to humdrum reality, only now something different was stirring up inside of me. It was a strange feeling, one that I can best describe as an inner tug-of-war and I knew that this was not something I was going to easily shake. Somehow, somewhere along the way, I had lost my sense of purpose in life and now it was as though I was being drawn to find it. Intuitively, I knew that I would no longer be able to just *go through the motions* anymore. What I didn't know was how I was going to change. As far as my faith was concerned, the only thing remotely reminiscent of it was the occasional Sunday mass and I was getting less and less out of that. I didn't have a clue where to begin. Most of the time, life itself seemed all for naught…if not one big oxymoron.

Don't get me wrong, it wasn't that I had taken an atheist point of view, I'd just been stagnant now for quite some time. While I believed that man had evolved over several thousand years, I disagreed with most popular evolutionary theories. Never would I entertain ideas that life was just a bunch of molecules thrown together by chance. Intellectually, emotionally, physically, and spiritually, I knew with no uncertainty that the universe, earth, nature, and life were all just a little too grandiose, too intricate, too awesome, and too marvelous to have happened by chance. Think about it, there are worlds inside of worlds! How incredible is that? I knew there had to be a Creator. So much of me wanted to believe in everything I'd learned as a child, but it was hard to when everyday life seemed *hell bent* on teaching me something else.

Somewhere I'd once read "when all else fails; follow life's instruction book" and next to this blurb was a picture of the Holy Bible. I thought I knew the Bible fairly well, but I had never actually sat down and read it entirely. If I was going to attempt to unfold some of life's mysteries and recapture my sense of purpose, this was a good place to start. Besides, this was the book that people of my faith swore by...literally. I wondered how our lives would stack up to it. Deep inside, I felt I already knew the answer.

My youngest brother, Mark, and his friend, Wendell, had visited me a year earlier and one of them left an international version of the Bible behind. Since I had no idea where my pocket version was, I decided this one must be here for a reason. As I brushed the dust off, a trail of questions arose in my mind. Is this the Word of God or the work of men? What part of it is parable and what part history? What part was subject to man's point of view and opinion? Did they get all the facts right? Is the Bible really the blueprint, the road map to follow? Is it as someone cleverly put it, an acronym for Basic Instructions Before Leaving Earth? I wasn't looking for theological arguments or some one else's interpretation as much as I was searching for *my* truth, so I didn't seek the counsel of anyone.

Shying away from the television, the telephone, and the myriad other technological interferences of the day, I began reading Scripture with no particular method to my madness; immersing myself nearly every night, stopping periodically to absorb certain passages, asking, "What is this really saying and how does this apply to me and the way life is today?" During this whole process, I was forced to examine the folly and mockery of my own life and I did not like what I saw. Through the years, I had allowed the real world to transform me from an extrovert to an introvert and from a lover of people to a loner. The real world taught me how to distrust and look out for numero uno. The real world had also taught me that it was acceptable to collect things and discard people. I'd come to believe that growing hard was a necessary part of self-preservation. Much like a song I used to listen to as a teenager..."*a child is born with a heart of gold...way of the world makes his heart grow cold.*"

Like many other people of my faith, when it came to really incorporating Christian values into my everyday life, I was only tapping on the surface. I had sufficient textbook knowledge from my early training, but I lacked any consistent practical application, ignoring those precepts I was violating in the same way that some people practice selective listening. Then, I justified my deviation by simply noting that everyone else I knew was deviating too. After all, who can understand a God that forgives and forgets, but is waiting to judge us according to our deeds? Who can understand that this same God whose love and mercy endures forever is a jealous and vengeful God? For goodness sake, how can you take the Bible literally when it says, *"if someone wants to sue you through law and take away your tunic, let him have your cloak as well."* Honestly, do you know anyone who does this in our dog-eat-dog, sue-happy society? Then there's, *"love your enemies, do good to those who hate you.... if someone strikes you on the right cheek, turn to him the other also."* Come on! At this stage, I'd even grown disenchanted with people who purported themselves as my friends, because often their insincerity and self-preoccupations told my heart otherwise. I always thought that a friend was someone that looks out for you, someone who really cares about your well being, and someone who's always ready to highlight your redeeming qualities, not someone who would smile in your face, then try to discredit you when you're not around. I had concluded a long time ago that my list of true friends was very short. Now, I was expected to love my enemies and turn the other cheek! To be quite candid, what went through my head as I read this passage was something like, "Yeah, well, I've got another pair of cheeks that they can all kiss!" It was obvious; the Word of God was in no way *living or active* in my heart.

Eventually, I got past some of my cynicism about the world around me and the skepticism I harbored about my faith. Sitting up in bed, reading Scripture with a candlelight flickering nearby became a sweet haven from the outside world. At times, the messages were too magnificent to comprehend, other times they spoke clearly and personally to me. I found myself lost in Proverbs 15:13 and 17:22...

*A happy heart makes the face cheerful, but a heartache crushes the spirit.*
*A cheerful heart is good medicine, but a crushed spirit, dries up the bones.*

So much time had passed since I'd felt the light-hearted glee of my youth. I didn't think it was possible for me to recapture that kind of optimism and joy, but I made up my mind right then and there to choose happiness and to focus on the sweeter things in life. Within a few weeks, I began feeling differently, lighter, calmer somehow. I still had many questions, but having all the answers didn't seem as pressing anymore. I found nothing in Scripture that required me to understand everything; it simply asked me to *believe.* I felt better about that.

There were times when the Bible seemed like a big satire exposing man's vices and stupidities and in the end or the beginning, however you choose to look at it, when *time* is up, God has a few proverbial "tricks up His sleeve," such as the last shall be first and the first shall be last. After reading Scripture, I felt spiritually nourished. Talk about revelations! I understood more than ever how foolish it was to call myself a Christian as I continued to go through life with such hypocrisy and indifference. The Bible confirmed for me how utterly meaningless it was to continually partake in religious practices when your heart was not in the right place. In other words, when such things as condescension, hatred, arrogance, separatism, un-forgiveness, jealousy, and malice are allowed to take up permanent residence in our *hearts*, rituals become exercises in futility.

A short time later, I gave up the no-longer-fulfilling, yet still-quite-stressful job. This meant, for the time being at least, that I also gave up a few luxuries I'd grown accustomed to. Judging from the response of others, they thought I'd gone stark raving mad or at least that I was acting irresponsibly. I didn't want to appear to be irresponsible; I was tired of the rat race. Sitting in an office with a view, pushing paper and peddling stuff I no longer believed in just didn't interest me anymore, even if I was earning a lot of money. I needed more time for introspection; I needed time to stop and smell the roses. And frankly, it really didn't matter how it looked to anyone else. I always thought that people were too eager to follow suit, rather than explore their own individuality anyway. You know how I feel about conformity for the sake of convention...yuk.

For years, it seemed the only time I really stopped was when I was asleep or stuck in traffic. The point is that when much of your life is spent crammed on a five-lane highway, you can easily miss out on the sweet fragrance of life. Oh, you get a scent all right, the smell of exhaust fumes mixed with a hint of road rage. To top it all off, I just didn't know how to unwind and relax anymore, let alone *be still and know God*. I figured a change would be healthy. So after sixteen years, I put my personal affairs in order, left the hustle and bustle of city life and headed for home on a nice sabbatical. Though most of the tales from my childhood turned out to be mythical and far-fetched at best, I thought at least Dorothy had it right, "there is no place like home." I soon learned firsthand that home can never be what it used to be as a child. Still, we all need this at some point you know, a kind of sojourn if you will…time to rest, time to pull away; time to put life in its proper perspective. Unfortunately, most of us aren't often able to pull away because of many demands and we become so routinely robotic that the only depth in our lives is what we see on the surface. We travel along life's highway with *no time* to ponder the true purpose of our existence; there's no clear exit to the path of enlightenment.

## NO TIME

I knelt to pray but not for long
I had too much to do
Must hurry off and get to work
For bills will soon be due
And so I said a hurried prayer
Jumped up from off my knees
My Christian duty now was done
My soul could be at ease

All through the day I had no time
To speak a word of cheer
No time to speak of Christ to friends
They'd laugh at me I feared
No time—no time, too much to do
That was my constant cry
No time to give to those in need
At last, t'was time to die

And when before the Lord I came
I stood with downcast eyes
Within His hand, He held a book
It was the 'Book of Life'
He looked into the book and said
"Your name I cannot find.
I was once going to write it down,
But I could not find the time."

-author unknown-

# THE PARADOX OF OUR TIME

The paradox of our time in history is that we have taller buildings but shorter tempers, wider freeways,
but narrower viewpoints
We spend more, but have less; we buy more but enjoy less
We have bigger houses and smaller families;
more conveniences but less time
We have more degrees but less sense; more knowledge,
but less judgment
More experts, yet more problems, more medicine,
but less wellness
We drink too much, smoke too much, spend to recklessly, laugh
too little
Drive too fast, get too angry, stay up too late, get up too tired,
read too little,
watch too much TV and pray too seldom.
We have multiplied our possessions, but reduced our values
We talk too much, love too seldom, and hate too often.
We've learned how to make a living but not a life
We have added years to our life, but not life to our years.
We've been all the way to the moon and back,
but we have trouble crossing the street to meet a new neighbor.
We have conquered outer space but not inner space
We've cleaned up the air, but polluted the soul
We've conquered the atom, but not our prejudice.
We write more, but learn less; we plan more, but accomplish less.
We have learned to rush, but not to wait.
We build computers to hold more information to produce more
copies than ever,

but we communicate less and less.
These are the times of fast foods and slow digestion; big men and small character
Steep profits and shallow relationships
These are the days of two incomes but more divorce, fancier houses but broken homes
These are the days of quick trips, disposable diapers, throwaway morality, one-night stands,
and pills that do everything from cheer to quiet to kill.
It is a time when there is much in the show window and nothing in the stockroom.
A time when technology can bring this message to you,
and a time when you can choose either to share this insight or to just hit delete.

Remember spend some time with your loved ones,
because they are not going to be around forever.
Remember say a kind word to someone who looks up to you in awe, because that little person will grow up and leave your side.
Remember to give a warm hug to the one next to you, because that is the only treasure you can give with your heart and it doesn't cost a cent.
Remember to say "I love you' to your partner and your loved ones, but most of all mean it.
A kiss and an embrace will mend hurt when it comes from deep inside of you.
Remember to hold hands and cherish the moment for some day that person will not be there again.
Give time to love, give time to speak,
give time to share the precious thoughts in your mind.

George Carlin, Author

In southwest Louisiana, people always want to know "who's your daddy?" Chances are, they know your people or they've heard of them. You might even find out that you're related, people are big into family and keeping track of their next of kin. Now this could be important if you're a young man calling on someone's daughter because in these parts, fourth and fifth cousins do count, even if they are twice removed, whatever that means. Then again, folklore has it that in some Louisiana coves, marrying your cousin may not have been so taboo after all. It's said that in these remote areas, folks did things a little differently to protect their land and sometimes their complexion.

As for my hometown, well it's a quaint, respectable little town, the kind of town where people rise to defend life and pro-life issues through the church. Yet, an unwed girl finding herself pregnant would undoubtedly feel the pressure to suffer an abortion rather than the stigma to her family, not to mention offsetting her plans for a bright future. It's a funny little town where people will take care to tell you not to drive bare feet, but it's legal to drive-thru and get frozen daiquiris to go. The locals' response to no drinking and driving campaigns is to tape down the lid of the to-go cup and not insert the straw. It's the kind of town where people will comment on your weight no matter how many times they see you in a week, as if you don't have a mirror at home. It's the kind of town where any news is big news and your business is everybody's business. So, you'd have to close your blinds just to change your mind. I guess in many respects, it's not that different from most little towns.

The area has grown quite a bit and the people here appear to be a lot more relaxed and comfortable with race relations.

Why is it then, that racial concerns are still among the hottest issues facing our schools? Half of a century has followed the Supreme Court ruling and still uncomfortable issues of segregation and racial balancing are on the front burner. One would think that after fifty years of trying to embrace integration, the people and government of this state, school administrators, and parents alike, would have a lot more profound and pressing issues to contend with. Yet here we are, well into the 21st century and it doesn't seem that many people, Black or White, have moved too far beyond feeling separate and different because of race. It just goes to show that you can change the laws governing segregation, but it doesn't change a thing, as long as people remain separate in their hearts. And in the end maybe it is a bit unrealistic to expect that separatism and racism could ever be eliminated in our lifetime, because all of it including slavery has been around since biblical times.

    The two old churches still operate separately except for the occasional interchange between Whites and Blacks. I guess that's why some folks say, "the more things change the more they stay the same." It didn't take long before I meandered inside of our seventy-five year old church for a few moments of quiet prayer. It's funny how buildings seem so much grander when you're a child. These days, the simple white, wooden structure with its steeple-front seemed much less overpowering. Once inside though, it was no less majestic. As nostalgia filled my senses, I was flooded with images of the old and familiar. It was as if I could still see Sister Marina at the door holding her pointer finger across her lips as she tried to line up fidgety kids to enter the church. That was her clear signal that we better hush and be reverent. When Sister Marina signaled, you definitely didn't want to miss it because the consequences were a little painful. My mind continued to travel back to a time of plaid uniforms and crisp white shirts, to the chanting on the playground and the yard-ruler spankings, to the aroma of delicious just-baked candy seeping from the convent, and the distinctive ring of the old school's hand held bell.

I didn't know how much time had elapsed as I sat in that rear pew, thinking about the way we were, and the way things were around us. Looking back, I guess it must have been comfortable for Whites in those days not to think about the impiety of having separate churches based solely on race. After all, there was nothing visible to remind any of us that Jesus was a Jew. The iconic Jesus we all adored had been completely Europeanized. I now know that it really doesn't matter what Jesus looks like, still I wondered why we couldn't have had a more authentic representation of Him and His culture. It's not enough to say that Jewish people never accepted Jesus as the Messiah, because this doesn't change the fact that He was a Jew; he certainly wasn't Roman.

A couple of years ago, I was floored when I read an article in our local newspaper written by a syndicated columnist out of Chicago. It was entitled, "New Look for Jesus in Television Series is a Makeover Gone Mad" The woman was attacking a series in which advanced computer programming was used to create an image of Jesus based on Palestinian-Jewish features during Jesus' time. She made some pretty narrow-minded remarks and blamed everything on biblical revisionists. Angrily, I wrote my own article in response, entitled "Jesus looks like all of Humanity." It went like this:

*Ms. Parker, I'm sure there was a valid point you were trying to make in your article, but I am still trying to find it. For God's sake and in His infinite wisdom, Jesus was born a Jew- among the poorest of the poor. By some historical accounts, His skin was brown, and He had hair like wool and feet of ash. With half a brain, one would know that geography and genealogy support this. So despite your childhood Bible storybooks, Jesus was never White with strawberry* blonde hair. Now that some are trying to develop what they think is a more realistic image of Him, you want to degrade it and call the nose depicted, 'a snout that snorts'. How would you feel if I said that based on your published photo, you have a pug nose that snoots? Sorry that you are having a hard time embracing what is probably a truer image of Jesus, but now you have a taste of how some non-White Christians have felt for years and years. As a Black child I was never taught that Jesus was a person of color, yet He was. As a Black child when we studied the Egyptians and the marvel of pyramids, not once did your books mention that Egypt is a part of Africa, yet it is. As a Black child, I was nearly 10 years old before I learned that in our household, Santa Claus was a Black man, and he still is! As a Christian of color, your article was an insult to me. Your message was much more dangerous than that of stupidity, it was a message of White supremacy—the old White is right. Well you are wrong! Your closing comment, though I hate to repeat it said, "Biblical revisionists won't be satisfied until they discover that Jesus was really a bi-sexual, cross-dressing, whale-saving, tobacco-hating vegetarian African Queen who actually went to the temple to lobby for women's rights." This is not only repugnant; it is sacrilege. Who are you or I to judge? God loves people who are unclear about their sexuality. He wants to mend and forgive. God loves the whales as He loves all living creatures; after all we are all His creations. God made tobacco and all produces of the earth are good; it's mankind's abuse that offends Him. God does want us to eat more vegetables...to get that lesson read Genesis 1:29 and Daniel 1:11-15. He didn't invent mad cow's disease; man did out of carelessness and greed. And if you look at countries like China, India and Africa, where in some parts, women are treated as sub-human; God probably is in favor of women's rights because these are basic human rights. Ms. Parker, why put God in a box? We were all made in His likeness and image. And if you are blessed to make it to heaven and you do get to see God; I hope that She has a beautiful, dark tan! In closing, I leave you with a biblical quote to ponder, I Samuel 16:7—" The Lord does not look at things that man looks at. Man looks at the outward appearance, but the Lord looks at the heart."

For me, the conflict over Jesus didn't stop there, not only

were many White Christians prejudiced against Blacks, there was a time when some were openly anti-Semitic too. How could you possibly hate Jews and worship one as your Lord and Savior? You can't have it both ways! Hatred and prejudice are not and have never been Christian values. At least now I can acknowledge that there is and probably always was, good clergy and good people in both church parishes in my little hometown. We were all just living in accordance with the times.

The Sisters that lived and worked in our parish when I was a little girl were called the Sisters of the Blessed Sacrament, an order of nuns founded by an amazing woman named Katharine Drexel. Born unto the wealthy banker and akin to the famous Bouvier family, Katharine Drexel of Philadelphia, PA, dedicated all of her adult life and her fortune to the education and progress of the Black and Native peoples of America. Had it not been for her, the majority of African Americans and Native Americans in the south during the early to mid 1900's would not have received an education, let alone a Christian one.

To my delight, I learned that Drexel built one of her schools on my grandparent's property in Prairie Bass, LA, in 1925. The property had been acquired years earlier through an Indian land grant by my great, great grandmother, whose tribal name was TonTon. A full-blooded Atakapa-Ishak Native American, TonTon was baptized and given the Christian name, Catharine Pierre. She was a popular medicine woman, a healer who treated the sick with infusions and poultices from plants and herbs. TonTon gathered her herbs near her home along the Vermillion Bayou, in Prairie Bass, LA. She was well known for her work and is mentioned in local historical writings that feature Indian Healers. The bridge near her home is still there and is to this day called the TonTon Bridge. My mother and her sisters and brothers all grew up on that land. Not only did they attend Drexel's school, some of them later taught at other Drexel schools.

# NATIVE AMERICAN 10 COMMANDMENTS

The earth is our Mother, care for her
Honor all your relations
Open your heart and soul to the Great Spirit
All life is sacred; treat all beings with respect
Take from the earth only what is needed and nothing more
Do what needs to be done for the good of all
Give constant thanks to the Great Spirit for each new day
Be honest and speak the truth; but only of the good in others
Take full responsibility for your actions
Enjoy life's journey, but leave no tracks

# NATIVE AMERICAN PRAYER

Oh Great Spirit, whose voice I hear in the winds
And whose breath gives life to all the world, hear me!

I am small and weak, I need your strength and wisdom.
Let me walk in beauty and make my eyes ever behold
the red and purple sunset.

Make my hands respect the things you have made
And my ears sharp to hear your voice. Make me wise
so that I may understand the things you have taught my people.

Let me learn the lessons you have hidden under
every leaf and rock. I seek strength,
not be greater than my brother,
but to fight my greatest enemy—myself.

Make me always ready to come to you
with clean hands and straight eyes. So when life fades,
as the fading sunset, may my spirit
come to you without shame.

In the 21st century, Drexel is known by some as the millionaire saint, but here in Assumption Parish in Carencro, LA, we like to think of her as our own. What I admire most about this great woman was her compassion and persistence. She had to be a smart and shrewd businesswoman to get things done in the south in the early 1900's. Drexel was very wealthy, so people were eager to do business or sell her their land, until they found out that she wanted to use it to build schools for Blacks and Indians; then, some of them wanted nothing to do with her. Katharine Drexel learned what not to say and do in attaining her goals and she accomplished them firmly and gracefully. The reason why I love and admire Katharine Drexel is because I, and so many others like me, am a direct beneficiary of her work. It's because of the groundwork she laid and the diligence and dedication of her Sisters that I am educated and can express my perspective with full confidence and commit it to paper. I know that Drexel must have encountered a lot of opposition, not just from strangers, but also from her own family and peers. Can you imagine their response to her mission? Can you imagine her subjecting herself to all that inconvenience and discomfort as she traveled to remote and desolate places to do most of the groundwork herself? Some say that in her mission she would conserve to the point that even a pencil she would not throw away until it was down to a stub. Can you imagine how easy it would have been for her as an heiress to take her multi-million dollar fortune and live a very, very comfortable life? Instead, she looked beyond her regal surroundings and saw her fellow man living in a despicable state of poverty and oppression and when no one was willing to step in, she did. Katharine Drexel didn't just talk the talk, she walked the walk. Because of this, she is one of my greatest heroes. Because of her, I have a modern day example of what it means to be a Christian. Through her life's work and the nuns who served us, I know for certain that the Word of God is indeed...*living and active.*

The portrait of Katharine Drexel that hangs at Acadian Village in Lafayette, LA, is an original portrait from the convent where the nuns resided at Assumption Parish in Carencro, LA. A photo of Katharine with my grandparents can be found in the archives at the Sisters of the Blessed Sacrament's motherhouse in Bensalem, PA. In October, 2000, with the Pope presiding, Katharine Drexel was canonized a saint by the Catholic Church at the Vatican in Rome, Italy. My mother, my sister Etta, several other family members and I attended the canonization. It was an extraordinary experience and one that I will never forget.

'Ours is the Spirit of the Eucharist...
the total gift of self.'

May your faith be increased
so that in all events of life,
in trials and sweetness,
sameness and changes,
you see in them but the workings
of Divine Providence.
May your faith be increased
so as to realize that you are never alone.
Wheresoever you may be,
the Great God is with you, in you.

Words of Katherine Drexel

A 21/25/0813

August 13, 1925

Prairie Basse School.

The Rev. Mother M. Katharine,
St. Elizabeth's,
Cornwells, Penna.

Dear Reverend Mother:-

The leader of the Prairie Basse Colored population has called to see me at my request, and was quite happy to learn that there is some chance of their having a school out there some time this year. I suggested that one of their men, who is competent for this work, go and look at St. Elisabeth's school near Carencro, and give me his figures for the construction of a similar school in Prairie Basse. I do not know whether it is your intention that the same kind of building should be put up there, but time is sopressing that I thought it well to take this step, whilst awaiting more definite instructions from you.

They tell me that the old shack on the place has been pulled down since you were out there because it was feared that it would be blown down as it was in very poor condition. The lumber was saved and put aside, that is, the larger pieces that could be used in the construction of the new school. This will mean some little saving in the price.

Would you be kind enough to let me know what size of building you would wish ? They assure me that there are over one hundred children of school age in that district.

Rumors have reached me that you were not quite satisfied with the way in which some of the new schools were being conducted; particularly in Rayne. If there is any foundation for these reports, dear Mother, I would be glad to know the nature of the grievance so as to be able to apply the remedy.

With blessing and all good wishes, I am,

Very devotedly in Christ,

Bishop of Lafayette.

*A letter from the Catholic Church Archives*
*Mentioning the property*

*Vintage photo of Katharine Drexel with my grandparents Washington Hayes Gordon and Andrea LeBlanc Gordon in 1925*

Within a short time of being home, I realized that the old neighborhoods hadn't changed much. Black children were still being tagged by the shade of their skin in the same natural way that you would describe someone as tall or short. I understand these references from older people because they grew up facing color and racial differentiating everyday; it was all they knew. I wish though that young people here would realize that they will always see skin color, yet to continually dwell on and call attention to it is a very shallow preoccupation. From my angle, this is no more than a remnant of slavery…like the old brown paper bag test. The bag was used as a benchmark, a point of reference from which you were decidedly lighter or darker. History tells us that slave owner, Willie Lynch advocated this kind of dissension among slaves as a method for continuing to divide and conquer them. I wonder if Lynch were alive today, if he would be proud to know that his legacy lives on in a peculiar kind of way. As long as it does, the colorful diversity that makes our heritage so flavorful, gives continued cause for separation rather than celebration. Author, Bell Hooks, invites young Black people to appreciate their natural beauty and to take pride in the physical attributes of our African heritage in her book *Happy to be Nappy*. The features of the White race should never have become the standard for Black beauty. What does it mean when Blacks are busy weaving in blond hair and sporting blue contact lenses? It means that European images are considered more attractive in this country and Blacks are becoming Europeanized. I'm not even going to get into Michael Jackson's skin color change and whether it was medically related or mentally related. The only observation I will share is that he was catapulted into a rich,

White world as a young boy and clearly, assimilation has its price. At least in the 60's and 70's, people of color vocalized Black pride and unity and saw beauty in afros and other physical traits of our African, West Indian and Caribbean ancestries.

On the other side of this, many Whites are busy tanning their bodies in every natural and unnatural way possible, often ignoring the risks of cancer. Nowadays blonde beauties inject foreign substances into their lips to make them fuller. Fuller lips are a physical trait of Africans, once considered highly unattractive in America, but is now considered sexy in Hollywood. Go figure.

In Black culture, there is a popular gesture of wearing gold plates on teeth. It's not exactly my idea of putting your money where your mouth is! I don't understand the logic or basis of this act, perhaps it has some implication to royalty, perhaps the practice is a relic of some ancient custom like tattooing. Today, both gold teeth and tattoos are a matter of choice and personal taste, but why would anyone choose to say "conversate" when the English language offers the word "converse". I don't know, but like the rest of the country, I have adopted the term, *bling*, to describe gold chains, medallions and other forms of ghetto opulence. Even linguists are beginning to embrace ebony phonics. I guess pretty soon, we'll all be hooked on *ebonics*.

Getting back on track, I have to admit, I had very little appreciation for Louisiana's unique culture when I left home years ago. I thought I was in a time warp the first time I heard "Tank ya cher" or "Mais jamais" or even better, "Dat's couillon yea." No, the people here are not illiterate, they are actually bi-lingual. And where else could you find English-French-speaking, Zydeco-dancing, crawfish-eating, beer-drinking, trail-riding, Black and White cowboys in this day and age? Only in southwest Louisiana!

In recent decades, the local Acadians have made quite a name for themselves with Cajun-style cooking and music. Their efforts have increased tourism and generated additional revenue for them and the state, so I say hooray for them. I know it has done a lot to improve their image because when I was a little girl the word *Cajun* was a negative slur used interchangeably with the term *coon-ass*. It wasn't always the 'in thing' to be. I also remember when Blacks were called *spooks* and that had a ghostly ring. And though I've never met him, I think Adolfo Harmon, a local activist, made a valid point when he was quoted by the Atlanta Journal as having said, "Acadians have sprinkled Cajun on everything like the dew; and with all-things-Cajun, the contributions made by Blacks and Creoles in this area have become obscured." This is a thought-provoking statement with which I am prepared to take issue.

I want my family and my people to appreciate and continue to validate the enormous contribution Blacks and Creoles have made to this area's growth and culture. The word *gumbo*, for instance, does not have Cajun roots. Gumbo is the Bantu name for okra, a vegetable indigenous to Africa. Bantus is a tribe in Africa whose name interestingly enough means mankind. We say gumbo, but in the old days, it was called Creole gumbo or file' gumbo and there were definite reasons for that. Today, gumbo is made with or without okra and with or without file' made from sassafras, but just pronouncing the word, you know it's not Cajun.

Recent work by Atakapa-Ishak descendant and author, Mr. Hubert Singleton, traces *jambalaya* back to its Native American roots. Mr. Singleton's extensive research substantiates that jambalaya is a word derivative adopted by Louisiana Spaniards. It was their phoneticized version of the phrase *Tsham pal a yah*, which literally means 'Be full, not empty. Eat up!' in Atakapa-

Ishak language. The dictionary of this language is preserved at the Smithsonian Institute.

By and large, many famous Louisiana dishes, including shrimp Creole, were created by Black cooks. Let's face it, Black people did most of the cooking in the south, during and since the time of slavery. We still have trademarked images like Aunt Jemima and Uncle Ben to remind us of this fact; so let's try not to forget it anytime soon.

The Colored and Black people of Louisiana have always been fluent in French and were able to communicate with Acadians since their migration. This was not Cajun French they were speaking. Blacks from the West Indies spoke the patois of their native land, Haitian Creole French. It is highly likely that imported Africans spoke French as well, due to the federation of French colonies in Equatorial Africa. Unfortunately, information like this is often disregarded or distorted in local historical accounts and the same thing holds true for the origins of Zydeco. The modern, popular dance in Louisiana may have derived from an Atakapa phrase *shi ishol*; translation: dance of the young. It is imperative that more people of color record their own family history, even if it's just short stories on a scratch pad or dicta-phone. It's also important that we support organizations whose primary mission is to acknowledge, appreciate, and preserve the Creole and Black culture of Louisiana.

A few years ago, the University of Louisiana at Lafayette, was celebrating its 100th year anniversary and several pioneers were being honored. My aunt, Christiana Gordon Smith, recognized as the first African American graduate from this university, was one of the honorees. This was a festive occasion, so facilitators were probably trying to steer clear of anything negative. They tended to gloss over the school's transition to include Blacks by saying that integration had gone smoothly with relatively no problems. I'm sure no misrepresentation was intended, but this is a matter of perspective. Mr. Ernest Gaines, a great author, renown for his literary works such as *The Autobiography of Miss Jane Pitman* and *A Lesson Before Dying*, was also an early graduate and an honoree at this celebration. He stood up, corrected the mistake, then proceeded to tell a little about the cruelties that he and early Blacks had endured as pioneers at this university. Thank you Mr. Gaines for telling it like it really was. History is history and it should not be rewritten so as to make the past appear different or less harsh than it really was. I also believe that this works both ways. I learned this from my Aunt Chris, a historian and dedicated teacher for nearly thirty years.

While still working, Aunt Chris was often asked to speak to groups about the history of Blacks in America and other subjects. I remember one MLK holiday, I went to hear her speak to a group of Black students and I was really caught off guard by some of the things she said. After discussing the unbearable conditions of slavery, she told the group that abolishing it could not have been accomplished without the help of White people. "What do you think made up the Underground Railroad?" she asked. Then she said, "Back then how many Black people do you think owned the barns and basements where runaway slaves could hide out on their journey to the north?" After a brief pause, she added, "White people helped to free Black people." Now this was an angle that I didn't often consider when I thought of slavery. I thank you Aunt Chris for your life's work and for broadening my point of view.

Today, there is an African American Alumni Chapter at this local university named in my Aunt Chris's honor. Among other things, annually it affords scholarships for aspiring Black students. And deservedly, a portrait of Christiana Gordon Smith now hangs in the university library.

Throughout my days, I've heard many revolting stories about how for generations, people of color were treated as if they had no hearts, minds, or souls. One of the most wrenching family stories that I recall was about my Uncle Johnny who was a veteran in WWII. The horror of the war left him injured and psychologically scarred. He was sent back from England to Virginia and placed in a medical facility for Whites. I assume at the time, they didn't know his race, as my Uncle Johnny was very fair. My Aunt Ludie, his sister, took a train to see him, but there were no rooms available at the hotel, so she thought she would stay at the military facility. When the officer looked at the papers she filled out, and saw that she marked "Colored." He told her that they could not accommodate her. She told the officer that the United States military didn't deny her brother from putting his life on the line as a Colored man, and asked why this was a problem now. Finally, another officer intervened, reasoning that since she had traveled all that distance to see her injured brother, they would give her accommodations.

Until I probed into that story, I didn't know that prisoners of war in America were allowed to enter main post exchanges and sit at the counters in cafeterias, and use the swimming facilities at military bases, when African American troops could not. Our own country was willing to send Black servicemen off to die on foreign soil to protect her, but was willing to treat the enemy with more dignity and respect. In spite of all that, Black and White men of our country bonded, fought, bled, and died together. As the old saying goes, two people you rarely find in a foxhole are a racist and an atheist.

That was years and years ago, but racial faux pas never seem to go away. Just a few months ago, my 13 year-old niece, Chincie, and I were sitting around after school chatting about homework, her dance recital, and life in general. Someone at school had told her that the reason why Blacks and Whites have the same last names is because slaves were given the last name of their masters as a way to track them, a mark of ownership so to speak. In Louisiana, quite a few Whites and Blacks share the same last names and a lot of these names are French in derivation, names like Mouton, Broussard, Thibodeaux and Angelle, just to name a few. As it is typical, the explanation that my niece got was only part of the whole story. With the succeeding generations of Blacks in this country, there were children born everywhere who were entitled to these surnames, if not by law, by blood. Sometimes they were entitled by both, as in this case.

In the early 1900's, my mother's aunt, Etta LeBlanc (pronounced Eè-tah in French) married a man named John Mouton, whose nickname was 'Dit' or Dick. Dick's parents were legally married; a Frenchman named Charles Mouton and a Haitian woman named Mathilde Scholl. It turns out that Charles' father was none other than Louisiana's notorious, first democratic governor Alexandre Mouton, which made my great Uncle Dick, Alexandre's legitimate grandson. There are legal records to substantiate this lineage at the local public courthouse and library. Whether or not the union of Charles and Mathilde was ever accepted by the elite family was a different matter all together. We think not because rumor has it that Charles requested to be buried with his wife upon his death; he was. Reportedly, later on though, one of his brothers moved his body to the White section of the cemetery where he belonged. So much for resting in peace! The fact remains that present day Blacks and Whites in Louisiana share common ancestry, as if this truth wasn't already self-evident. Common surnames weren't acquired only through slave ownership; there was a lot of co-mingling going on. One author, Carl A. Brasseaux, did an awesome job of describing that in his book, *The Founding of the New Acadia*, published in 1987. Brasseaux, a descendant of French settlers in Louisiana, boldly noted that, "The intensity of the Acadian-Creole feud can be partially attributed to amorous affairs between Acadian men and Creole women. The interest of Creole men in slave women is indicated by the emergence of significant Mulatto population...." His research also reinforced the fact that famous Louisiana cuisine has West Indies and African origins.

Lalita Tademy, author of the popular book *Cane River* tells a poignant personal story that touches a sensitive nerve of many who read it because for Creole families, it is a familiar family saga. Nearly twenty years before Tademy's testimony, Gary B. Mills authored *The Forgotten People* in 1977. Mills embraced the daunting task of tracing the history of some of the Creoles of Cane River and highlighting the social and political significance of the color caste system, which permeated Louisiana since the antebellum period. It is a well-researched account depicting how Blacks were viewed as sub-human in those eras and how the degree of black blood one had in them was measured and tracked down to a fraction. Every native of Louisiana, and for that matter, America, would do well to read it as a valued part of our nation's history.

The discomfort surrounding race and color was a big part of why I left the Deep South as a young adult. Now that I had returned, it was the very thing that I was having a hard time getting re-acclimated to. It's obvious that some strides have been made and there are a lot of beautiful people here both Black and White, who have worked to tear down the walls of separatism. Too many other people convince themselves that they aren't racist because they're not involved in overtly drastic measures like lynching or bombing. Racism comes in many forms and can be quite subtle if not second nature. It occurs every time a so-called good, church-going person consciously or unconsciously chooses not to sit next to someone who is of a different race. It occurs every time a White person sees a young Black man driving an expensive car and assumes he must dealing drugs. The media, Hollywood movies, and rap music videos all help to perpetuate this misconceived image. Racism occurs every time a Black person thinks that all Whites are exploitive and rage against them for no specific reason. It occurs every time the right person is passed up for a job or promotion just because of some ethnic attribute. Racism is something that evolves when people believe they are essentially superior solely because of their race or skin color. In fact, I would venture to say that every time you see color and that causes you not to see the person, it's a form of racism. Perhaps the only thing more damaging and dangerous than racism itself is the pretense that it doesn't exist anymore.

Certain mindsets are deeply ingrained here in southwest Louisiana, allowing little advancement in the way people think from one generation to the next. Attitudes are planted as firmly as those little ceramic Black butlers that were placed outside of White people's homes as decor for roughly a century. Whenever I contemplate the Deep South, I do so with mixed emotions. Suffice it to say that some things that should have *gone with the wind*, simply did not go.

# EXCERPT FROM NELSON MANDELA'S INAUGURAL SPEECH, 1994

Our deepest fear is not that we are inadequate.
Our deepest fear is that we are powerful beyond measure.
It is our light, not our darkness that most frightens us.

We ask ourselves, who am I to be brilliant,
gorgeous, talented and fabulous? Actually, who
are we not to be?

Your playing small doesn't serve the world.
There is nothing enlightened about shrinking so
that other people won't feel insecure around you.

We were born to make manifest the glory that
is within us. It's not just for some of us, it's in
everyone. And as we let our own light shine, we
unconsciously give other people permission to do
the same. As we are liberated from our own fear,
our presence automatically liberates others.

Today, I better understand that hatred, prejudice, and ignorance are not confined to the south; they permeate this country and stretch out to the remote corners of the world. Since the terrorist attacks on September 11th, this has become even more apparent to me than ever before. Racial profiling and hate crimes quickly emerged against Arabs and sheik-types, shifting the stereotype from "driving while Black" to "flying while Arab." I guess any excuse will do to hate. In the name of security, some people went so far as to say that we shouldn't allow any more foreigners into the United States. I agree that there needs to be control to discourage aliens from flooding in illegally. But I got a newsflash for Americans: we're *all* foreigners or descendants of foreigners, save the few full-blooded Native Americans still alive today.

Everywhere one turned, American flags were waving and red, white, and blue signs were proclaiming, "God Bless America," "One Nation Under God" and "In God We Trust." It appeared that our faith and patriotism had been restored. Yet, everywhere one turns today, legislation is on the table to take prayer out of schools, out of football games, and if we remain complacent enough, someone will pull God right out of our pledge of allegiance. Where exactly are we going with this? Why would we renounce everything that the forefathers who shaped the new America stood for? Even with their imperfections, they took care to put God in everything from our constitution to our currency. They didn't seem to be too concerned with separation of church and state. In fact, in the Declaration of *Independence*, these forefathers openly declared their *dependence* on the Supreme Justice of the world. I believe that because of this, God has been the source of this country's strength, protection, and greatness.

It used to be customary to place the right hand on the Bible in court, when swearing to tell the truth, the whole truth and nothing but the truth. Somewhere along the way though, we stopped that custom and somewhere in this country today, someone wants to remove a stone depicting the Ten Commandments, simply because it sits in front of a courthouse.

It would stand to reason that this insistent movement away from prayer and the Divine Providence could only lead this nation to one destination…its demise. Once again, the American people are called upon to draw from the ideals we say we believe in or continue to be traitors to everything this country stands for.

President Bush appeared to be doing a fine job helping the nation to recover. So much so that even Democrats like me had all but forgotten about those ugly little *dimpled chads* that seemed to diminish our confidence in the voting process in Florida, this past election. But even during the 9-11 recovery period, there were more incongruent messages to decipher. Our federal government was basically telling us to be on the highest alert for repeat attacks and in the next breath, entreating us to get on with our lives as usual. We were leading a war where we were bombing the country of Afghanistan while simultaneously supplying its people with food.

Today, countries are fighting everywhere, nation against nation. Psychics, projectionists, and prophets are predicting it's the beginning of the end of times. Needless to say, I look for comic relief wherever I can find it. My cousin Milton Jackson, who we affectionately call June, can always be counted on for a good laugh. He was just telling me how his wife, Cyn was upset with him for not stopping the car so she could give money to a beggar on the side of the road. June is a good-natured, giving person, but he was laughing so hard he could barely get the words out when he mustered, "Look here cuz, I don't feel guilty at all, that Negro was wearing a beeper and carrying a cell phone, he couldn't possibly have been that hungry."

Touché! It's a sad and beautiful world.

Ultimately, we each have to choose for ourselves what's important in this whole human experience. Strangely, I find that I don't value much of what most of my peers seem to value at this stage in my life. I guess each person's model of the world is based on that person's individual experiences and the interpretation of those experiences. Reflecting back now, I see that adversity has had its purpose in my life. After the initial shock, anger, and disappointment, adversity and suffering caused me to search for deeper meaning to life and eventually brought me closer to God. Hardship stripped me of any false pride and arrogance I may have embodied and moved me towards humility and compassion for others. Today, I thank God for His wisdom. Of course, I am only human, so I wouldn't intentionally choose to hurt or experience pain, but without setbacks and loss in my life, I could have been well on my way to being a shallow, self-important person unable to find value in every human life, like too many people I know. As someone knowledgeably said, 'we think too much of ourselves when we think too little of God.'

I believe God allows extraordinary events to occur in ordinary lives for a much grander purpose, even if while you're living it, it feels like a nightmare. Later on, those experiences might be used as a blessing in someone else's life. My heroes are women with a strong *will*. All of them, throughout history, from Mary, the mother of Jesus, to Mother Theresa; from my ancestor Catharine Pierre to Katharine Drexel; from Harriet Tubman to Eleanor Roosevelt. I have male heroes too, but I can relate to strong self-sufficient women, probably because there are so many in my present and ancestral family. My present day heroines are women who met adversity head on, tackled it to the ground and then proceeded to flow through life with grace, dignity, and fortitude: women like Maya Angelou, Tina Turner, Oprah Winfrey, Myrlie Evers-Williams, and yes, the unconventional Vanessa Williams. I admire any woman with the courage to take a horrific life experience and demonstrate something powerful and good from it. It's said that into every life some rain must fall, perhaps this is how we come to fully appreciate the glory of the sun. These women have taught me that it's not so much what life brings to you, rather what you bring to life that counts.

## WILL

There is no chance, no destiny, no fate
can circumvent or hinder or control
the firm resolve of a determined soul.
Gifts count for little; will alone is great;
all things give way before it, soon or late.
What obstacle can stay the mighty force
of the sea-seeking river in its course,
or cause the ascending orb of day to wait?
Each well-born soul must win what it deserves.
Let the fool prate of luck.
The fortunate is one whose earnest purpose never swerves,
Whose slightest action or inaction serves…
the one great aim.
Why, even death stands still…
and waits an hour for such a will.

Ella W. Wilcox
1850

Mom and Dad are enjoying life as they should be...50+ years of marriage is a rare find nowadays. One has to admire them for having accomplished so much with so little to start with. Both born into big close-knit families, they were each the ninth child of ten. I like to sit and have coffee with them and chuckle at their "If it ain't hurtin, it ain't workin" repertoire on the aches and pains of aging. In their early seventies now and semi-retired, my parents are still getting more done before 9 a.m. than I seem to accomplish all day. As much as I have tried to give back in my own way, they still manage to do more for me than I could ever do for them.

Our father, Whitney Peter Mouton, Sr. has had many trades in his lifetime. Today, he still enjoys growing crops and raising cattle. As a young man, he served in the Navy. There he worked in the kitchen and his love for cooking began. The Navy afforded him an opportunity to see many parts of the world that he might otherwise have not been privy to during that time. He must have had a big taste of it, because he won't travel for long distances these days unless he feels he has to. He says he just doesn't care for all that rigmarole anymore.

As a young man, Whitney courted Lela before going into the service. He'd been in the Navy for about six months and was going by train from New Orleans to San Diego when he met a lady on the train who was getting off in Lafayette, LA. He asked her to deliver something to his girlfriend and paid for the lady's cab fare. It was Lela's engagement ring! My parents were married in Norfolk, Virginia, in 1947.

Daddy's siblings include Ward, Loomis, Wilma, Earl, Doris, Irene, Herman, Harold, and Gloria; some of them are deceased at the time of this writing. Their father, Alphey Mouton was the son of Alphonse Mouton and Mama Celeste. Alphey attended Tuskegee Industrial School in Alabama back in the early 1900's, studying agriculture and shoe repairing. Proprietary work was quite progressive for a Black man in the South back then. It must have rubbed off because Daddy and his brothers were all entrepreneurial in spirit. In the fifties, they owned and operated a nightclub called the Avalon Grill in Opelousas, LA. His brother, Earl later owned another business, the Hollywood Inn. Daddy shared his father's love for business and for turning the soil of the earth. To this day, he absolutely loves his garden and it is always bursting with plump vegetables and melons. Oftentimes, he strolls slowly up and down the isles with his hands clasped together behind him, thinking or praying, sometimes just to get away from the chatter in the house. This is clearly his place of solace and he grows a crop every year with a good demand for his crisp white okra. He is very generous with his produce and one of the many ways God blesses Daddy's generosity is that his garden is always overflowing. God continues to bless him and he continues to bless others with those blessings. He is an awesome cook too. Daddy believes that when it gets quiet at the dinner table, it's a compliment to the chef because people are so busy eating they don't have time to speak. With all the fresh vegetables and fresh beef at our fingertips, it was no secret that we kids lived "high on the hog" and sometimes Daddy would laugh when he'd tell his buddies, "Man, these Negroes eat like kings."

Dad's mother, Mary Greene Mouton, worked from sun up to sun down because of the many chores demanded of women during those days without modern conveniences. Her family remembers her as a gentle and good woman who worked at home and lived for her children. She liked to listen to soap operas by radio, like *Amanda on the Honey Moon Hill* as she whisked and worked throughout the day. Mary's mother was part Indian, but we are not sure which tribe. There are good indicators however, that it was Attakapa-Ishak. Her father, Jimmy Greene, was African American and part Irish. Jimmy had moved to Louisiana from Virginia years earlier. As a carpenter, he helped build churches in Arnaudville and Cecilia, LA. Daddy undoubtedly took a lot from his parents because he's always worked hard. Even at 74, he still believes in an honest day's work.

Our father is well known in this little town and his friends come to visit him regularly and have a sip of coffee. He saves his toddies for his good friend, Mr. August and cousin Loomis, and gladly lets them know when it's their time to replenish. He's known as 'Mout' and, though he's no politician, he once served as Councilman. He doesn't believe me when I tell him that he is one of the smartest men I know, but it's awesome the way he can do math in his head. If he can't remember some minor detail, he says sourly that he's slipping. I assure him that as long as he can still account for every penny of his diversified investments and every penny still owed to him by anyone in his head, he is not slipping.

Daddy is the rugged outdoor type with a big heart, though you wouldn't know it from his facial expression these days; he would be frowning right now if he knew I was writing about him. Every morning at 5 a.m., you'll find him in his favorite chair praying the rosary. As you can see, he doesn't have any hang-ups about women in high places and we should know, our mother is a strong matriarchal force in the household.

Mama was born Mary Lela Gordon and her siblings include Ludie, Emery, Charlie, Annabelle, Christiana, Rita, Johnny, Leroy and Imelda. Some are deceased at the time of this writing. Mama is an active, Eucharistic Minister, Lector, and

Choir Member in our church. She has served on various boards and commissions in the Catholic Diocese. She takes her faith seriously. If you're going to sleep over at her house on Saturday, you're going to church on Sunday, so bring your church clothes.

Through the years, I've watched our mother care for and bring gifts to the elderly and sick in the community. She is my greatest example of practicing what you preach. How she found special time for each and every one of her children through the years is still a mystery to me, but she manages to be strong and gentle at the same time; a tidy blend of warrior and southern belle. Daddy may not like to travel much, but Mama still loves to go. She always travels throughout the country for different occasions, like the birth and baptism of a grandchild or a graduation. When she's around the house she loves to bake. You can't refute the aroma of her pecan, sweet potato or blackberry pies. Other than that she routinely sterilizes everything and lives by Lysol and Listerine. Mama enjoys tinkering in her flowerbeds and, like Daddy, everything she touches just blossoms. At 73, she has just completed her first computer class. She also loves to read books, solve crossword puzzles, and outwit contestants on TV game shows, especially Wheel of Fortune and Jeopardy. She jokingly tells people that Daddy may be the head of the household, but she is definitely the neck!

Proud of all her roots, Mama will be the first to let you know that acknowledging your entire lineage, is not selling out and she openly defends Tiger Woods on this issue. Andrea LeBlanc Gordon, my mother's mother, was half French and half Native American. She died when her children were fairly young. She was a devout Christian who prayed often, cared for and helped clean the nearby chapel, and picked fresh flowers daily for the altar. Wise and well-liked, local teachers and priests looked up to Andrea and they often came to visit with her, sometimes even seeking her counsel. She, like my other grandmother, did it all; early in the morning she pumped drinking water from the well, scooped up eggs from the chicken coop and milked the cows. And that was just to get breakfast going!

Adopting some of the healing methods of her Indian background, Andrea made poultices from herbs. She developed an herb potion to treat worms that was later patented. It was called Red Cross Medicine, but she was never recognized or paid by the doctor who touted her discovery. As a traiture or treateur (a French term for someone who treats sick people), Andrea believed in combining prayer in the form of chanting, with her herbal remedies.

Mama's father was Washington Hayes Gordon. He ran a blacksmith shop, filing plows and other tools for the field workers. He was a farmer by trade too and sometimes worked at the sugar cane factory in a little village called Ruth Plantation. Washington played the mandolin, in fact all of the Gordon men from that generation and the next, played musical instruments. They were self-taught and played by ear; Mama said it was in their blood. Washington's father was part Irish or Scottish. There are conflicting reports, but the revealing traits are red hair and freckles. His mother was from the West Indies.

TonTon was my mother's great grandmother on her mother's side. A full-blooded Atakapa-Ishak Indian, TonTon was considered a free woman of color, which basically meant she wasn't White and she wasn't a slave. Very few pureblooded Native Americans can be found today in Louisiana, but they are not as extinct as some people would have you believe. Some Indians married White and their children went that way, while some married Black and their children went that way. It is reported that the few pure Atakapa-Ishak Indians still alive today are living near the Lake Charles area. A recent publication on Louisiana Indians claims that people of the Atakapa-Ishak Tribe were cannibals. My research shows no real evidence of that, except that they may have been exercising a Native American ritual where they took a tiny piece of their enemy after killing or burning them, thus symbolizing power gained over that enemy.

My parents have seen a lot of changes in their days. They have lived through the days of out-houses, horse-and -buggies, and picking cotton. I am proud to say that they are still independent and going strong in this new age of modernization and technology.

Through the passing years, our family has been through a lot together. We're a big family, so in addition to many joys and successes, we have also had to deal with our share of sadness and hardships too. Families are made up of imperfect members who have differing views and priorities. The one common and cohesive ingredient is love. We have learned from our father, the head of our big clan, that we have to stick together. There will always be forces out there to try and rip a family apart. At times, it isn't always easy to know the right thing to do in a particular situation, especially when you don't want to condone a certain behavior yet you don't want to condemn a loved one. I'm sure we don't always get it right, but one thing holds true: there is no greater anchor in life than to have the love and support of a strong family. Come what may, we will not be divided because a family that prays together stays together.

In the early years of our marriage, we prayed the selfish prayer of...

## GIVE US

And you answered Lord, you gave us eight children and the health
and ways to earn a living to sustain them.

Then we prayed the prayer of...

## FORGIVE US

Because as many young people do, we made mistakes through the years.
We acknowledged them and were sure you heard our prayer.

## MAKE US

We pray as we grow older that you make us worthy of you. Lord, make us models of your son, Jesus, to emulate him in all we do and say in this world. And finally Lord we ask you to...

## TAKE US

We pray Lord that at the end you take us to your heavenly home where there will be no more tears, pain or worry and that someday our family will be reunited with you, Mary and Joseph, The Holy Family forever and ever.

Your Prodigal Children,
Whitney & Lela Mouton
Golden Anniversary / March 6, 1997

# A MOTHER'S PRAYERS

When you are absent from the Lord and the wickedness of your lying lips show in your eyes

Wondering why your breath has not been shortened, or your bones been broken, or why harm has not come to you

It's your mother's prayers

It seems there is no end to the evil doing
But you have not been blemished
Yet your sleep is restless and your dream is of your enemies,
But they have not snared you in their net.

It's your mother's prayers

Whenever little things seem to have fallen on you
Yet you get from under them

It your mother's prayers

For God has made a covenant with her
For if she believes in Him and all His righteousness,
All her offspring will be saved from harm's way

Thank God for mothers' prayers

Written by my brother
Peter W. Mouton

Well, I'm a long way from the starry-eyed optimist of my youth, but at least I'm not just *going through the motions* anymore. These days, I try to surround myself with things that foster healing and growth, and people who allow me to feel good about being *me*. I like to take long walks down windy roads, pick herbs and wildflowers, and sometimes plop under a big oak tree with a good book; the kind of luxuries city life can seldom afford. I continue to read the Bible and other books about life, faith, and spirituality. I believe that meditative prayer, an open mind and heart, exposure to other ways of thinking, and varied life experiences are ways that we evolve, acquire wisdom, and ultimately find our purpose and who we really are.

To say that my life has been an oxymoron is no overstatement. Not only has it been full of contradiction, but also the more I know, the more I realize how much I don't know, much like a *wise fool*, hence, the oxy and the moron. One thing I do know is that I don't want to be a hypocrite all of my life, so I don't plan to spend the rest of my days chasing the wind. There are still so many personal areas that I want to improve on. As I continue to at least try and live the values that I believe are so important and move away from the many secular magnets in the world, I've learned not to look for any fan mail. It just doesn't add up to success in most people's eyes and keeping up appearances is so important in our world.

The new generation of my family has so much more than the last. Our children have every kind of material possession imaginable, every electronic gadget that comes out on the market, expensive designer clothes, and more money to spend on consumable nothings than ever before. Don't get me wrong, I think prosperity and six-digit incomes are great, I just hope our kids don't attach *all* of life's value to just those things, because there is so much more to life, so much more than meets the eye.

My godchild, J.D., and another nephew, B.K., were here visiting this past summer from Georgia. They are both little intellects in their own right who love to outwit their parents and teachers. A couple of years ago, I started a little consulting practice and I bought a little efficiency car to keep my expenses down. One day, I was taking them to the video store, and as soon as J.D. got in the car, he immediately wanted to know where the power button was so he could put the window down. I told him the power was in his hand and that he could turn the knob anytime he was ready. You should have seen his face as he stared at it. I don't think he had ever seen one before, but at least he was well-mannered enough to say, "It's a cute little car, Nanny." B.K. on the other hand was open-minded enough to admit that he'd seen a turn-handle knob before in his Dad's old secondary work truck!

There is so much pressure in our culture to display our wealth or perceived wealth. I think my nephews felt a bit sorry for me because they thought I was poor. Oddly, though they were young, I felt sorry for them because they couldn't see the riches I was seeking…wisdom, knowledge, and truth. *Wisdom is a shelter as money is a shelter, but the advantage of knowledge is this: that wisdom preserves the life of its possessor. Ecclesiastes 7:12.* Throughout my life, I never want to live vicariously through someone else's life, idea of life or through someone else's accomplishments. I just want to be me and self-actualization is my victory! I'll know that I have truly arrived when I am no longer concerned with the opinion of others to validate me, or my choices. Sometimes in life one has to take a few steps back to be able to leap forward. And sometimes less…is more.

I believe there is in each and every one of us, whether we are red, yellow, black, or white, a spark of the Infinite Goodness that created us, that Great Light. I believe that when we leave this earth we merge as one with the Light because we are *one* and we *all* make up the Light. What you do while you are here on earth, how well you learn to love, and help others without gain, may very well determine how bright *your* ray of Light will shine for all eternity.

*More perspective and biblical reflections...*

# Physical Appearances

A wise person once said, 'Pulchritude possesses solely cutaneous profundity.' Today, we know this little idiom as, 'physical beauty is only skin-deep.' If it has a noble ring to it, it's probably because we all know that outward appearances serve not to reflect the heart or soul. While it may be humanly natural to want to be attractive, the grave importance placed on this in our society should be alarming. Undoubtedly, this growing vanity is going to cost us in more ways than one. We used to accept that beauty and youth were fleeting. Now, beauty is a technologically advanced commodity bought and sold every day in a multi-billion dollar cosmetic industry. Miracles in a jar claim to work magic tricks, but if those aren't magical enough, surgical laser genies can nip and cut, lift and tuck. Cosmetic surgery has permeated our culture so deeply that it's not unusual for a teenage girl to ask her parents for a little rhinoplasty or breast implants in lieu of a birthday party, and get it! Today's teens are only following the lead of millions of adults who get on the cutting board each year to the tune of ten billion dollars.

Have we become too shallow to appreciate that natural beauty comes in all shapes and sizes? Beauty was once in the eyes of the beholder, but today it is redefined through youthful, emaciated images projected by the media. The American population alone spends in excess of thirty billion dollars annually on diet food, diet pills, diet books, and diet programs. In a land that imparts little tolerance and lots of heckles for overweight people, we tolerate senseless diseases like bulimia and anorexia as natural by-products of our thin-ness fixation. And after all of this money and malady, we still manage to have one of the highest obesity rates in the world. To top it all off, the demand for scientifically formulated, anti-aging, anti-wrinkling potions continues to explode at a phenomenal pace. Some are so desperate they actually have *botulism toxins* or *botox*, injected into their faces to eliminate wrinkles! So it's not surprising that one of the highest compliments you can give someone today is to say, 'you don't look your age.' As usual, all is not what it appears to be; no one's really turning back the hands of time. It seems that in the long run, we have completely lost sight of virtuous sentiments like 'inner beauty' and 'aging gracefully.' Ancient civilizations revered their elderly for their tenure and wisdom. Where is the progress of an advanced civilization that seldom celebrates its seniors, but is rather preoccupied with avoiding the idea of aging all together?

---

## ISAIAH 53:2
He had no beauty or majesty to attract us to him, nothing in his appearance that we should desire him.

## GALATIANS 2:6
As for those who seemed to be important- whatever they were makes no difference to me; God does not judge by external appearance- those men added nothing to my message.

## I SAMUEL 16:7
The Lord does not look at the things that man looks at. Man looks at the outward appearance, but the Lord looks at the heart.

## PROVERBS 27:19
As water reflects a face, so a man's heart reflects the man.

## JOHN 7:24
Stop judging by mere appearances, and make a right judgment.

## LEVITICUS 17:13
Rise in the presence of the aged, show respect for the elderly and revere your God. I am the Lord.

## PRAYER
Lord, when I lose touch, please remind me that it is what's on the inside that counts. In lieu of a face-lift, I lift my heart to You.

# Money and Materialism...

America is known as the land of opportunity where rags to riches stories do come true. It's a bountiful land that continues to deliver on the promise of great prosperity. America is also a land of great disparity too, and along the great economic divide the more wealth you've got, the more you're admired. Success is measured mostly in dollars and cents, the sum of our great love affair with opulence. In this country, we bow to the rich and famous and scramble to rub elbows with movie stars and celebrities. We automatically deem pro ball players as role models for our children, not for their philanthropy or sportsmanship, but rather because they get paid millions of dollars to hit a ball with their hand, foot or a stick. That's far more than our teachers and leaders earn and we entrust our children's futures to them.

More money gives us more choices and comfort, so who wouldn't want to be 'livin large?' The idea alone lures some to engage in unscrupulous endeavors, while the lives of social climbers revolve around status symbols in keeping up with the 'Jones.' Our nation's most un-talked about social disease is *'affluenza'*- the compelling desire to be rich, to be among the affluent. Unfortunately, instead of landing in the lap of luxury, many find themselves lost in a financial maze laden with debt. We're a nation of spenders and consumers, not savers and investors. And thanks to our mixed-up value system, when the net-worth dwindles, the sense of self-worth dwindles too. Dr. Martin Luther King, Jr. once said eloquently, " We have bowed before the god of money, only to learn that there are such things as love and friendship that money cannot buy and that in a world of possible depressions, stock market crashes and bad business investments; money is a rather uncertain deity. Transitory gods are not able to save or bring happiness to the human heart. Only God is able. It is faith in Him that we must rediscover."

## Matthew 6:19
Do not store up for yourselves treasures on earth, where moth and rust destroy, and where thieves break in and steal. But store up for yourselves, treasures in heaven where moth and rust do not destroy and where thieves do not break in and steal.

## Ecclesiastes 6:3
Whoever loves money, never has money enough.

## Luke 12:14
Then he said to them, "Watch out for all kinds of greed; a man's life does not consist in the abundance of his possessions."

## Proverbs 23: 4
Do not wear yourself out to get rich; have the wisdom to show restraint, cast but a glance at riches and they are gone.

## Matthew 19:24
"Again I tell you, it is easier for a camel to go through the eye of a needle than for a rich man to enter the kingdom of God."

## Luke 16:14
The Pharisees, who loved money, heard all this and were sneering at Jesus. He said to them, "You are the ones who justify yourselves in the eyes of men, but God knows your hearts. What is highly valued among men is detestable in God's sight.

## Jeremiah 29:11
"For I know the plans I have for you" declares the Lord, "plans

to prosper you and not to harm you, plans to give you hope and a future."

## Prayer

Lord teach me the secret of being content whether I am living in plenty or in want; for I know there is no advantage for me to gain the whole world and yet forfeit my very self…my soul.

# Food and Health...

Little grandmothers were known to say, "An apple a day, keeps the doctor away." It was a simple little prescription for good health. But granny's apples weren't sprayed with harmful pesticides, forced ripe, then artificially dyed and waxed to look deep red. Today's apples might not produce quite the same results, because what you see isn't always what you get. It's amazing how we Americans claim to be health conscience while consuming vast amounts of animal meats, starchy side dishes, and sugar-surging desserts, a riddle in itself. A typical day's diet consists of over-processed food in a box...fast food, frozen food, canned food, instant food, and dehydrated food. Our reasoning: the hustle and bustle of hectic lives demands convenience. Advertisers take free reign with food claims, telling us their products are all natural and healthy as they lace them with monosodium glutamate, silicon dioxide and yellow dye #9. So daily, we consume anti-caking and binding agents, fillers, preservatives, and dyes, along with their lies.

Everything we need for a healthier existence is graciously supplied by nature: water, vegetables, fruit, grains, nuts, plants, and herbs. The human body is an inimitable marvel with an innate capacity to heal itself, though we test it to its limits. We have tested the earth; even our water so essential to our existence we have carelessly contaminated. We pour trash into our bodies as though they were waste dumpsites, then we expect these same bodies to continue to be vital and resilient. We consume and waste more food than any other continent on the planet with no real regard for global hunger. Fellow human beings are actually starving to death and we collectively think that it's not our problem. So, grandma how ya' like them apples?

## Genesis 1:29
Then God said, I give you every seed-bearing plant on the face of the whole earth and every tree that has fruit with seed in it. They will be yours for food.

## Daniel 1:11-13
Please test your servants for ten days. Give us nothing but vegetables to eat and water to drink. Then compare our appearance with that of the young men who eat the royal food....at they end of 10 days, they (servants) looked healthier and better nourished than any of the young men who ate the royal food.

## Matthew 15:11
"What goes into a man's mouth does not make him 'unclean', but what comes out of his mouth, that is what makes him 'unclean.'"

## James 2:15
Suppose a brother or sister is without clothes and daily food. If one of you says, "Go, I wish you well, keep warm and well fed" and does nothing about his physical needs, what good is it?

## Proverbs 22:9
A generous man will himself be blessed, for he shares his food with the poor.

## Prayer
Oh Creator, thank You for the bountiful gifts from Mother Nature. Show me what I can do personally to close the gap between world waste and world hunger.

# Nature and Healing...

Too many of us look to any miracle pill prescribed by the medical profession to instantaneously fix what we have in some cases taken years to break. And a gainful medical industry is more than happy to oblige our hypochondria. We trust them implicitly all the while ignoring the long list of side effects accompanied by most synthetically manufactured drugs. Of course, people who have serious conditions require the expertise of qualified doctors and the advancements of modern medicine, which have helped to sustain countless lives. It doesn't take a brain surgeon to figure out that a little self-care beforehand, costs much less than damage control later. Little grandmother's also said, 'an ounce of prevention is worth a pound of cure.'

We've increased our dependency on a profit-making industry to fix us, re-make us and supply us with wonder drugs. Who are the real winners when one ailment is alleviated at the expense of introducing several more? They are! Since this profession has been slow to embrace holistic healing methods, a good number of people assume that natural remedies are primitive and ineffective. A closer look reveals that the use of natural nutrients and herbs will never be as lucrative as developing and dispensing wonder drugs. Only the pharmaceutical manufacturers who legally push drugs like Prozac, Viagra and Ritalin at exorbitant prices can give us the bottom line on that. No sooner than we removed alcohol and cigarette advertisements from TV, and here comes the drugs- generating billions of dollars in annual revenues for these companies, black market figures not included!

Long ago, Native Americans and other aborigines throughout the world instinctively knew the medicinal benefits of plants indigenous to their lands. They were one with the earth cherishing it for its gifts. Today, opportunists have exploited this area too-sometimes cheating us out of the very essential herb they are touting. Still, we can't afford to ignore what nature has to offer in its simplest and purest form. Even the lowly regarded dandelion wildflower commonly found growing in yards has hidden healing properties. It's a natural cleansing tonic and helpful in detoxifying the liver, not to mention high in potassium, iron, and vitamins. Yet, interestingly enough, we buy weed killer to destroy the dandelion because it upsets our lawns, and then we turn around and pay more money for artificial vitamins and nutrients off the shelf. Perhaps God sprinkled the earth with dandelions for a reason, along with a myriad other miraculous, healing plants and herbs.

---

## SIRACH 38:4-8
God makes the earth yield healing herbs, which the wise one will not neglect. There is no end to the Lord's creative work, which spreads health over the whole world.

## EZEKIEL 46:12
Their fruit will serve for food and their leaves for healing.

## PSALM 103:2-3
Praise the Lord, O my soul, and forget not all His benefits- who forgives all your sins and heals all your diseases.

## PROVERBS 4:22
For they are life to those who find them and health to a man's whole body. (The Word of God)

## PRAYER
Lord, thank You for gifts of health and healing. Please bless and guide all medical professionals, caretakers and healers who give

of themselves for others. I pray that health care can once again be about people, not profits.

# Words and Speaking…

"Sticks and stones may break my bones, but words will never hurt me" was the popular line we chanted as kids. It was like having ammunition at your beck and call to retaliate against any kind of name-calling. As the words flowed from your lips, you already knew that you'd reached for them in pain. Speaking is such a natural part of our interaction with others that we often don't give our words a second thought. Sadly, some people don't give their words a first thought. The old "think before you speak" cliché has real merit especially when one is hurt or angry and tempted to lash out. Through one's choice of words we can see how enthusiasm is exuded, and through another's choice of words just how much misery loves company. Words give us the ability to uplift another's spirit or tear it down. Who would want to be accountable to God for someone's broken spirit? Yes, speaking is a great power that we possess…one that is largely underestimated.

Adults say "children should be seen and not heard," perhaps that's why we teach our kids to speak when they are spoken to. Still others argue that it's better to remain silent and be presumed ignorant, than to speak and remove all doubt. Chatterboxes claim to have the gift of gab, but it may not be a gift after all—because after all is said and done, more is said than done. When we choose our words carefully and used them frugally, it allows more time for thinking and doing. To our benefit, this would leave less time for gossiping. At its best, gossiping is half-knowing and whole-telling a story. At its worst a snooper's scoop is full of elasticity and harmful intent. Distinguished first lady, Eleanor Roosevelt cleverly summed it up by saying, "Great minds discuss ideas; average minds discuss events; small minds discuss people."

## Ephesians 4:29
Do not let any unwholesome talk come out of your mouths, but only what is helpful for the building of others up according to their needs, that it may benefit those who listen.

## Matthew 12:34-36 & Luke 6:45
For out of the overflow of the heart the mouth speaks. The good man brings good things out of the good stored up in him, and the evil man brings out the evil stored up in him. But I tell you that men will have to give account on the day of judgment for every careless word they have spoken. For by your words you will be acquitted, and by your words you will be condemned.

## Proverbs 12:18
Reckless words pierce like a sword, but the tongue of the wise brings healing.

## Proverbs 13:3
He who guards his lips guards his life, but he who speaks rashly will come to ruin.

## Proverbs 26:22
The words of a gossip are like choice morsels, they go down to a man's inmost parts.

## Proverbs 10:18
He who conceals his hatred has lying lips, and whoever spreads slander is a fool.

## Jeremiah 9:5
Friend deceives friend, and no one speaks the truth. They have taught their tongues to lie; they weary themselves with sinning.

## Prayer
Silent meditation on the boundless love and mercy, which pours from the heart of Jesus…Guard my lips Oh Lord!

# Work and Corporate Culture...

In the 21st century, the concept of 'job security' gives one a very insecure feeling. No, you'll never hear the phrase 'permanent position' in the workplace again. Apparently, we can expect to see the continued pattern of mergers between big companies driven by power and greed, that unquenchable thirst for greater profits—the notorious bottom line. Yes, this is largely what has made America great! If free enterprise, healthy competition and stable jobs are components of that greatness then why do we seem to be moving away from them? Why are big corporations transforming into giant conglomerates closely resembling, but never actually called monopolies? These mega-entities say they are better able to serve as they hide further and further behind sophisticated telecommunication systems. The name of the game is increase profits and shareholder earnings, whatever the cost, even if it's illusive...as in 'cooking the books.' But in the case of mergers, those at the bottom appear to be paying the biggest price of all, as corporate marriages of these kinds invariably cost jobs. Downsizing after upsizing didn't sound politically correct, so it's been reframed nicely as right-sizing, reorganizing or restructuring. No matter what label companies put on it, the results are the same: suits perched behind mahogany desks discard people as surplus, disrupting and re-arranging their lives with the mere stroke of a pen.

The blatant loss of value for human capital in the workplace cultivates an atmosphere of uncertainty and distrust for those who remain behind to hold up the fort. All the while, 'good ole boy' networks and office politics are going strong as EEOC compliance pledges are proudly displayed in highly visible areas. This promotes a collective clear conscience and in turn helps to mask the inequities; which indeed exist. For many workers, the glass ceiling is more like a brick wall, but what can they do about it? Mostly, fear the consequences that might result from confronting unfair corporate practices. Employees are held hostage due to thirty-year mortgages and other family obligations. Whatever happened to the loyalty once shared by both employer and employee? For that matter, whatever happened to good old fashion 'elbow grease'? By and large, people of America still need challenging, stable employment that will provide a sense of security. Regrettably, a lot of people want a job but not a lot of them want to work.

## COLOSSIANS 3:23
Whatever you do, work at it with all your heart as though working for the Lord, not for men…It is the Lord Christ you are serving.

## PROVERBS 12:24
Diligent hands will rule, but laziness ends in slave labor.

## PSALM 37:7
Be still before the Lord and wait patiently for Him; do not fret when men succeed in their ways, when they carry out their wicked schemes.

## PROVERBS 10:16
The wages of the righteous bring them life, but the income of the wicked brings them punishment.

## I THESSALONIANS 4:10
Make it your ambition to lead a quiet life, to mind your own business and to work with your hands just as we told you, so that your daily life may win the respect of outsiders and so that you will not be dependent on anybody.

## Prayer

Lord, guide me in my daily work life that I may be diligent and above board in all of my affairs. Give strength and wisdom to all of those working in religious and missionary vocations.

# Unity & Separatist Thinking...

With only one great omnipotent God—one Source for mankind, one Author of life, it's hard to imagine so many different beliefs to choose from. Yet, faith is as colorful and as diverse on this earth as the human species, which walks the face of it. From Christians and Jews to Hindus, Muslims and Buddhists; we all have a kinship with God. There is no call to be narrow-minded and think that our Creator who made us all, doesn't love us all. You don't have to agree with differences to respect them. Even within Christianity, spin-off religions evolved because someone thought differently. So we don't agree on everything; does that justify the assertive attacks that are prevalent between religious groups? In the end, aren't we all trying to get to the same place? Some people can't even begin to embody love and acceptance within their own church, let alone outside of it. People actually go to church to find Jesus, but they have a hard time sitting next to someone who is different. They may avoid offering a stranger the sign of peace in the form of a handshake, then leave without ever realizing that they just rejected the very One they came to see. Church is about fellowship with one another as One Body. God is about unity not separatism. Not just with respect to church, it's the way we carry out our separate little lives everyday. And those Christians who live life as though it were a contest to see how much they can outdo others materially, now they have missed the ark completely. Life is not a contest. Jesus said and demonstrated time and time again that we are one. So that should tell us that when we hurt someone else; we hurt ourselves, and when we help someone else, we help ourselves. If the profound meaning of 'oneness' would truly resonate deep within us, we would understand the everlasting gravity of our interactions with each other, and then how differently we would treat one another...how differently we would all carry out our lives.

---

## MATTHEW 25:40
The King will reply, 'I tell you the truth, whatever you did for one of the least of these brothers of mine, you did for me.'

## MATTHEW 25:45
He will reply, 'I tell you the truth, whatever you did not do for one of the least of these, you did not do for me'.

## EPHESIANS 4:4-6
Make every effort to keep the unity of the Spirit through the bond of peace. There is one body and one Spirit- just as you were called to one hope when you were called- one Lord, one faith, one baptism, one God and Father of all, who is over all and through all and in all.

## TITUS 3:9-11
...avoid foolish controversies and genealogies and arguments and quarrels about the law, because these are unprofitable and useless.

## I CORINTHIANS 12:12-13
The body is a unit; though it is made up of many parts; and though all of its parts are many, they form one body. So it is with Christ. For we were all baptized by the one Spirit into one body—whether Jews or Greeks, slave or free- and we were all given the one Spirit to drink.

## ROMANS 12:4
Just as each of us has one body with many members, and these

members do not all have the same function, so in Christ we who are many form one body, and each member belongs to all the others.

## Psalm 133:1
How good and pleasant it is when brothers live together in unity!

## Prayer
Lord, sometimes I think you must be frustrated with us on this, because it's so simple and we are so petty. Teach us all to truly accept one another and to love each other as one.

# Pride and Humility...

The 'high and mighty' tend to take an elevated view of the world from their pedestals, peering down on those who don't fit into their class, whatever they perceive that to be money, power, title, genealogy, even ideology. They aren't born with silver spoons in their mouths or their noses stuck in the air, they arrive in this world like everyone else, naked and without possession. They will leave here just as everyone else will, with only the works of the soul. Pompous attitudes and snobbish behavior have an awkward place in faith-filled lives. How can we possibly be filled with compassion for others when we're so full of ourselves? We are stewards of God's gifts not permanent owners and when we forget that through Him all graces flow, gratitude steps out and selfish pride is allowed to grow.

Modesty towards self and mildness towards others are subtle ways that we can acknowledge God. Besides, self-exaltation is redundant when success speaks for itself. Too many 'high horses' on this carousel of life, makes things a little top-heavy. Humility is an important, intrinsic facet of our faith, one that is often ignored or misunderstood. After all, who would choose to be among the meek and lowly in a world that caters to the proud and lofty? Very few, that's who. Thank goodness in this lifetime we were blessed to have Mother Theresa of Calcutta as a living testament to the great height of humility. She lived a quiet and gentle life serving the poorest of the poor, ultimately becoming a giant through her caring and humble ways.

---

## James 3:13
Who is wise and understanding among you? Let him show it

by his good life, by deeds done in humility that comes from wisdom.

## Isaiah 2:12
The Lord Almighty has a day in store for all the proud and lofty, for all that is exalted, they will be humbled.

## Romans 12:3
For by the grace given me I say to everyone of you: Do not think of yourself more highly than you ought, but rather think of yourself with sober judgment, in accordance with the measure of faith God has given you.

## Romans 12:16
Live in harmony with one another, do not be proud but be willing to associate with people of low position. Do not be conceited.

## Proverbs 16:5
The Lord detests all the proud at heart. Be sure of this: they will not go unpunished.

## I Corinthians 1:31
Therefore as it is written: "Let him who boasts boast in the Lord."

## Philippians 2:3-4
Do nothing out of vainful conceit or selfish ambition but in humility consider others better than yourself.

## Ephesians 4:32
Be kind and compassionate to one another.

## PRAYER
Emmanuel -God with us, You washed the feet of Your disciples! Because of Your example I desire a humble and contrite heart.

# Suffering & Hardships...

When suffering enters our lives, we make feeble attempts to make human sense of it. We witness our friends or neighbors having problems or experiencing setbacks and we sometimes stand in judgment. People are quick to proclaim that we reap what we sow. To a large degree, our free will, choices and decisions do affect and shape our lives. Are trials and tribulations always the resulting consequences of our actions? We cannot explain it anymore than we can explain why some babies are born into wealth and health and others are born into starvation and sickness; why some are born onto loving, nurturing parents and others are born onto abusive or neglectful ones. Surely these innocent young creatures are not guilty of any wrong doings.

How many of us fully trust in God's divine plan during despair? How easy is it to walk by faith during times of adversity? Do you know anyone who rejoices in their sufferings with the perfect knowledge that they are sharing in Christ's sorrowful passion? More than likely during hard times we feel unjustly treated, cheated by God somehow. We could all learn from a remarkable woman named Francis Crosby, a gifted songstress whose works, like *Blessed Assurance*, are still enjoyed today. Despite the fact that Francis lost her sight at birth due to a doctor's error, she wrote inspiring lyrics and remained joyful throughout her life to the point of saying, "It seemed intended by the blessed Providence of God that I should be blind all my life, and I thank Him for that dispensation." In scripture we find that God does not ask us to understand, He asks us to believe! Perhaps we should finally conclude as a faithful Job did after enduring immense suffering and trying to make sense of it before God; admit that we speak of things we do not understand, things too wonderful for us to know.

## JAMES 5:13
Is anyone of you in trouble? He should pray.

## PROVERBS 19:3
A man's own folly ruins his life, yet his heart rages against the Lord.

## ROMANS 5:3
...but we also rejoice in our sufferings, because we know that suffering produces perseverance; perseverance, character; and character, hope...and hope does not disappoint us...

## HEBREWS 2:10
In bringing many sons to glory, it was fitting that God, for whom and through whom everything exists, should make the author of their salvation perfect through suffering.

## ISAIAH 53:3
He was despised and rejected by men, a man of sorrows and familiar with suffering.

## JAMES 1:2
Consider it pure joy, my brothers, whenever you face trials of many kinds.

## JOB 42:3
You ask, 'Who is this that obscures my council without knowledge?' Surely I spoke of things I did not understand, things to wonderful to know.

## PRAYER
Jesus, You once felt abandoned by God and wept. Teach me to

accept that my times of sadness, like yours, are filled with the hidden presence of our Father's love.

# Love & Relationships...

'What the world needs now is love- sweet love; it's the only thing that there is just too little of.' More melodies have been written about amorè than any other theme in the world it seems. Yet we never seem to have quite enough of it to go around. Maybe it's because when it comes to love we don't always say what we mean or mean what we say. We seek physical affection and we call this love. We seek security and we call this love. We seek monetary comfort and we call this love. Thus, it stands to reason that when we say someone has 'married well;' this has nothing to do with love. Our needs and desires are often misrepresented as love. True love gives of itself and seeks *nothing* in return, and people just don't operate that way. If love is synonymous with God and we're made in His likeness and image, it's the stuff we're made of. Love is our true essence. Scripture tells us to love the Lord our God with all our hearts, to love our neighbors as ourselves and to love our enemies, because love conquers all.

The word love or some variation of it, is mentioned more than six hundred times in the Bible. So we know we're supposed to love, but still it's just not exactly free flowing from our hearts. Perhaps, because of past hurts, perhaps because of the biases and hang-ups we've collected along the way, perhaps because we're so busy feigning love that we wouldn't recognize it if it was staring us in the face. Nonetheless, everybody needs love. An old church hymn resounded, 'God is love and he who abides in love, abides in God and God in him.' Love is the atonement for any wrong we've done, but it needs to be hands-on in our lives and shown through our deeds and actions. Love should be up close and personal, not just something aesthetically pleasing to say or hear, because when it comes to love, one thing is for sure, actions speak louder than words.

## I John 3:19
Dear children, let us not love with words or tongue but with actions and in truth.

## I Peter 4:8
Love covers over a multitude of sin.

## Luke 7:47
Therefore I tell you, her many sins have been forgiven—for she loved much.

## I John 4:7-8
Dear friends, let us love one another, for love comes from God. Everyone who loves has been born of God and knows God. Whoever does not love, does not know God, because God is love.

## I John 4:16
God is love. Whoever lives in love, lives in God and God in him.

## Roman 13:10
Love is the fulfillment of the Law.

## Matthew 24: 12-13
Because of the increase of wickedness, the love of most will grow cold, but he who stands firm will be saved.

## Prayer
Lord, help me to look past unimportant things so that I can truly love. Oh before I forget, I love You!

# HAPPILY EVER AFTER...

At a very tender age, children are tossed into a mystical world of fantasy, a world full of magic wands, flying carpets, and castles; 'once upon a time' fairy tales weaving life into a wonderland adventure until they all live happily ever after. In those early years, life seems to offer no clear distinction between the world of reality and the world of make-believe. Most of us clumsily stumble on to the truth, as we discover there is no tooth fairy, no Easter bunny, and even Santa Claus isn't who he's claimed to be. Still, we wouldn't trade these fanciful characters for anything in the world. As young adults, we're told to reach for the moon, for the sky is the limit, and so starry-eyed we set out with lofty goals and high expectations. Throughout life, there are some wonderful times and great successes, but we experience setbacks and disappointments too. Real life outcomes aren't always easy to accept, especially when you've been conditioned to utopian endings.

Gradually, we are disrobed of our romantic fantasies and begin to accept that life is not a picture-perfect fairy tale. There's no prince to ride off into the sunset with, no sleeping beauty to awaken, and even the old silver lining begins to look suspiciously like aluminum foil. This is a time when many of us become so disenchanted with life that we stop reaching for magnificence and start settling for mediocrity, smugly calling this new standard, facing reality! But, facing reality should never mean giving up hope, and there is always the hope of living happily ever after. It's God's gift of eternity. If only we could truly fathom a harmonious infinite life where time has no purpose and evil has no presence, we might all be more mindful of this gift. Instead, we focus mostly on temporal and visible things, the physical and the material.

## Proverbs 19:21
Many are the plans of a man's heart, but it is the Lord's purpose that prevails.

## I John 2:25
And this is what he promised us—even eternal life.

## Titus 1: 2
A faith and knowledge resting on the hope of eternal life, which God, who does not lie, promised before the beginning of time.

## Ecclesiastes 3: 10-11
I have seen the burden God has laid on men. He has made everything beautiful in its time. He has also set eternity in the hearts of men, yet they cannot fathom what God has done from beginning to end.

## 1 Thessalonians 5:16-17
For the Lord himself will come down from heaven, with a loud command, with the voice of the archangel and with the trumpet call of God, and the dead of Christ will rise first.

## 2 Corinthians 4:18
Therefore we do not loose heart…for our light and momentary troubles are achieving for us an eternal glory that far outweighs them all. So we fix our eyes not on what is seen, but what is unseen. For what is seen is temporary, but what is unseen is eternal.

## Prayer
Lord, help me to not loose heart during times of trouble no mat-

ter how unfair they may seem. Oh Prince of Peace, I long to live happily ever after with you.

## Matthew 7:12

So in everything, do to others what you would have them do to you, for this sums up the Law and the Prophets.

# ACKNOWLEDGEMENTS

There are so many special people who have touched my life in extraordinary ways and I'd like to acknowledge a few of them:

My Aunt T-Glo and Aunt Irene, thanks for always being so sweet to me, and in memory of Aunt Nan,.. oh how I miss your lemonade!

My Aunt Chris, you may not have been able to finish your book due to health reasons, but God only knows the work that you poured into it. This one's for you too. Aunt Rita, Aunt Annabelle and Aunt Imelda, I love you.

My Uncle Leroy Gordon of Mercer Island, WA. Thank you for always being kind and giving me positive encouragement. And to all my uncles, I love you.

Sister Isaac Jogues aka Mary Ellen Monnat of Rochester, NY, you have been one of my greatest teachers. Thank you and all the nuns for giving up so much of your lives for us. Your work was not in vain.

Terry J. Celestine and David 'Mickey' Williams, who left our world too soon. You will never be forgotten.

Ginny, a grief counselor who came to me like an angel at the lowest point of my life, God bless you, wherever you are.

Debra and Alvin Matthews of Oakland, CA, for promising the least and giving the most when we needed it most.

The Pearsons of Ventura, CA. Alma, Kit, Arlene and Mark thank you for receiving me as a part of your family...oh and you too Andrew.

Dr. Felice O' Ryan, for being such a competent professional and caring human being.

Sister Monica for the healing graces I received through your spiritual work with herbs and Reiki.

Denni Cravins, my friend and younger kindred spirit. I've learned so much from you so I know wisdom is not just a function of age. Thank you for helping me to refine this work. Never lose your spirit of compassion and truth.

My sister Etta, thank you for taking the time to help me refine this work. Your efforts are not unappreciated.

Marcella Senegal and your beautiful daughter Hannah—you know you're my girls!

Juleigh Wiltshime, you don't know me, but your name is printed in the Bible that has served me so well. I'd like to get it back to you.

Musical artists, India Arie and CeCe Winan for lifting my spirit with your music; and Ali McGraw for elevating my mind with her Yoga: Mind, Body and Soul, workout video.

All of my friends at Chevron Oil Company in the Bay

Area of California and at National Data Corporation in Atlanta…I miss you.

All the famous and not so famous people that I quoted throughout this book, and those who shared their poems and writings. To the teachers, motivational speakers, ministers and priests whose lectures and works through the years, inspired some of the writings in this book.

To you Lord…my power source!